Best Garden Plants *for* OHIO

Debra Knapke • Alison Beck

Lone Pine Publishing International

The Distributor: Lone Pine Publishing
1808 B Street NW, Suite 140
Auburn, WA, USA 98001
Website: www.lonepinepublishing.com

Library and Archives Canada Cataloguing in Publication

Knapke, Debra, 1955–
    Best garden plants for Ohio / Debra Knapke, Alison Beck.

Includes index.

ISBN-13: 978-1-55105-496-4
ISBN-10: 1-55105-496-5

    1. Plants, Ornamental—Ohio. 2. Gardening—Ohio.
I. Beck, Alison, 1971– II. Title.

SB453.2.O3K53 2006   635.9'09771   C2005–906169–3

Scanning & Electronic Film: Elite Lithographers Co.

Front cover photographs by Tamara Eder and Tim Matheson except where noted. *Clockwise from top right:* flowering crabapple, flowering cherry, bearded iris, lilac, daylily 'Dewey Roquemore,' sweet potato vine, daylily 'Janet Gayle' (Allison Penko), lily (Laura Peters), dahlia, lily (Erika Flatt)

Photography: All photos by Tim Matheson, Tamara Eder, Laura Peters and Allison Penko except: David Austin Roses 106; Bailey Nursery Roses 105a; Doris Baucom 162a; Sandra Bit 133a; Conard-Pyle Roses 105b, 107a; Joan de Grey 42a; Don Doucette 100b&c; Derek Fell 61a, 95a, 145a&b; Erika Flatt 9b, 85a, 128b; Saxon Holt 61b, 109a, 157; Horticolor (G4500059) 119b; Jackson & Perkins 115; Duncan Kelbaugh 128a; Liz Klose 164a, 165a&b; Dawn Loewen 69a, 97b; Kim O'Leary 87a, 127a, 131a, 140b; Photos.com 134a; Robert Ritchie 37a&b, 40a, 43a, 51a&b, 63b, 77a&b, 80a, 91a, 104a, 113a, 121a, 140a; Gene Sasse-Weeks Roses 107b; Leila Sidi 134b; Joy Spurr 119a; Peter Thompstone 19a, 46a, 47a, 55a&b, 57a, 169b; Mark Turner 95b; Don Williamson 121b, 130a&b, 136a; Tim Wood 63a.

This book is not intended as a 'how-to' guide for eating garden plants. No plant or plant extract should be consumed unless you are certain of its identity and toxicity and of your potential for allergic reactions.

PC: P13

Table of Contents

Introduction

Starting a garden can seem like a daunting task, but doing so is an exciting and rewarding adventure. With so many plants to choose from, the challenge is deciding which ones and how many you can include in your garden. This book is intended to give beginning gardeners the information they need to start planning and planting gardens of their own. It describes a wide variety of plants and provides their basic description, planting and growing information and tips for use to get you started producing a beautiful and functional landscape.

Ohio has a temperate climate; the summer growing season is long and warm, and winters are cold enough to ensure a good period of dormancy and plenty of flowers in spring. Rainfall is fairly predictable, with heavier rains in spring and fall and an extended hot period with less rain from July through September. Winter snowfall varies from good snowcover in the northeastern and southeastern part of the state to 'sleetfalls' in the central and southwestern regions. The soils can be anything from a sandy loam to a silty clay, and they support a variety of healthy plants.

Hardiness zones and frost dates are two terms often used when discussing climate and gardening. Hardiness zones are based on the minimum average winter temperatures over a given period of time. Plants are rated based on the zones in which they grow successfully. The last frost date in spring combined with the first frost date in fall allows us to predict the length of the growing season and gives us an idea of when we can begin planting out in spring.

Microclimates are small areas that are generally warmer or colder than the surrounding area. Buildings, fences, trees and other large structures can provide extra shelter in winter, and they may also trap heat in summer, thus creating a warmer microclimate. The bottoms of hills are usually colder than the tops, but they may not be as windy. Take advantage of these microclimates when you plan your garden and choose your plants; you may even grow out-of-zone plants successfully in a warm, sheltered location.

Getting Started

When planning your garden, start with a quick analysis of the garden as it is now. Plants have differing requirements, so it is better to put the right plant in the right place rather than try to change the soil, the light conditions or the form of the land to suit the plants you want.

Knowing which parts of your garden receive the most and least amounts of sunlight will help you choose the proper plants and decide where to plant them. The amount of sun a site receives is generally described with the following terms: full sun (direct, unobstructed for more than six hours), partial shade or partial sun (direct sun for four to five hours per day and shade for the rest), light shade (shade all or most of the day, with some sun filtering through to ground level) and full shade (no direct sunlight). Most plants prefer a specific amount of light, but many can adapt to a range of light levels.

The soil is the foundation of a good garden. Plants use the soil to hold themselves upright, but they also rely on the many resources it holds: air, water, nutrients, organic matter and a host of microbes. The soil's structure, which depends on the particle sizes it contains, influences the amount of air, water and nutrients it can hold. Sand, with the largest particles, has lots of air space and allows water and nutrients to drain quickly. Clay, with the smallest particles, is high in nutrients but has very little air space. Water is therefore slow to penetrate clay and slow to drain from it.

Soil acidity or alkalinity (measured on the pH scale) influences the amount and type of nutrients available to plants. A pH of 7 is neutral; a lower pH is more acidic. Most plants prefer a soil with a pH of 5.5–7.5. Soil-testing kits are available at most garden centers, and soil samples can be sent to testing facilities

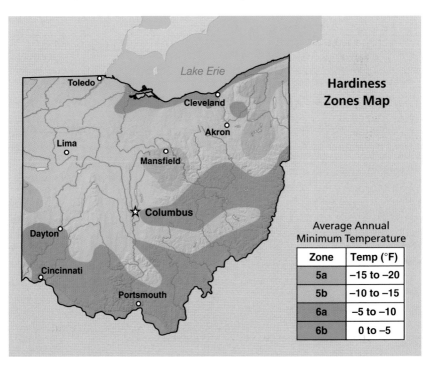

Hardiness Zones Map

Average Annual Minimum Temperature

Zone	Temp (°F)
5a	−15 to −20
5b	−10 to −15
6a	−5 to −10
6b	0 to −5

for a more thorough analysis. Knowing the pH of your soil gives you an idea of what plants will do well in your garden and what amendments you might need to add.

Compost is one of the best and most important amendments you can add to any type of soil. Compost improves soil by adding organic matter and nutrients, introducing soil microbes, increasing water retention and improving drainage. Compost can be purchased, or you can make it in your own backyard.

Selecting Plants

It's important to purchase healthy plants that are free of pests and diseases. Such plants will establish quickly in your garden and won't introduce problems that may spread to other plants. You should have a good idea of what the plant is supposed to look like—its habit and the color and shape of its leaves—and then inspect the plant for signs of disease or insect damage.

The majority of plants available at nurseries and greenhouses are container-grown. It is an efficient way to grow plants, but plants grown in a restricted space for too long can become pot bound, with their roots densely encircling the inside of the pot. The pot can often be carefully removed temporarily to check for girdling or pot-bound roots, rotten roots and soil-borne insects. Roots wrapping densely around the inside of a pot must be lightly pruned or teased apart before planting. Avoid purchasing pot-bound plants, because they are often stressed and can take longer to establish. Plants that have a dense mat of roots growing out of the pot may need to be coddled once planted.

Planting Basics

The following tips apply to all plants.

* Prepare the garden before planting. Remove weeds, add any needed amendments, such as compost or manure, and, if possible, dig or till the soil in preparation for planting. These preparations may be more difficult in established beds to which you want to add a single plant. The prepared area should be the expected size of the plant's root system on maturity.

* Know the mature size. Plant based on how big plants will grow rather than how big they are when you plant them. Large plants should have enough room to mature without interfering with walls, roof overhangs, power lines, walkways and surrounding plants.

* Unwrap the roots. It is best to remove any container before planting to give roots the chance to spread out naturally when planted. In particular, you should remove plastic containers, fiber pots, wire and burlap before planting trees. Fiber pots decompose very slowly, if at all, and wick moisture away

1. Gently remove container.

2. Ensure proper planting depth.

3. Backfill with soil.

from the plant. Burlap may be synthetic, which won't decompose, and wire can eventually strangle the roots as they mature. The only exceptions to this rule are the peat pots and pellets used to start annuals and vegetables; they decompose and can be planted with the young transplants. Even these peat pots should be sliced down the sides, and any of the pot that will be exposed above ground should be removed to prevent water from being wicked away from the roots.

• Accommodate the rootball. For planting herbaceous plants into a prepared bed or border, your planting hole only needs to be big enough to accommodate the rootball with the roots spread out slightly. Otherwise an area big enough to accommodate the mature root system should be prepared. For woody plants, the hole should be one and one-half times the width and exactly the depth of the rootball. Do not dig up the soil that will be below the rootball, or the plant may sink, causing problems.

• Plant at the same depth. Most plants like to grow at a specific level in relation to the soil and should be planted at the same level they were at in the pot or container before you transplanted them.

• Settle the soil gently. Good contact between the roots and the soil is important, but if you press the soil down too firmly, as often happens when you step on the soil, you can cause compaction, which reduces the movement of water through the soil and leaves very few air spaces. Instead, firm the soil around the newly placed plant with light hand pressure. Then water the area thoroughly. The water will settle the soil evenly without allowing it to compact.

• Identify your plants. Keep track of what's what in your garden by putting a tag next to each plant when you plant it. A gardening journal is also a great place to list the plants you have and where you planted them. It is very easy for beginning and seasoned gardeners alike to forget exactly what they planted and where they planted it.

• Water deeply. For most plants, it's better to water deeply once every week or two than to water lightly several times per week. Deep and thorough watering forces roots to grow as they search for water and helps them survive dry spells when water bans may restrict your watering regime. Always check the root zone before you water, because some soils hold water more effectively than others. More gardeners overwater than underwater. Mulching helps retain moisture and reduces watering needs. Containers are the watering exception—they can quickly dry out and may even need daily watering.

4. Settle backfilled soil with water.

5. Water the plant well.

6. Add a layer of mulch.

Choosing plants

When choosing your plants, aim for a variety of sizes, shapes, textures, features and blooming times. Features such as decorative fruit, variegated or colorful leaves, seedheads, unusual forms and interesting bark provide interest when the plants aren't blooming. This approach results in a garden that is captivating year-round.

Annuals

Annuals are planted anew each year and are expected to last only for a single growing season. Their flowers and decorative foliage provide bright splashes of color and can fill in spaces around immature trees, shrubs and perennials.

Annuals are easy to plant and are usually sold in small cell-packs of four or six. The roots quickly fill the space in these small packs, so the small rootball should be broken up before planting. I often split the ball in two up the center or run my thumb up each side to break up the roots.

Many annuals are grown from seed and can be started directly in the garden once the soil begins to warm up.

Trees and shrubs provide backbone to the mixed border.

Perennials

Perennials grow for three or more years. They usually die back to the ground each fall and send up new shoots in spring, although some are evergreen or semi-shrubby. They often have a shorter period of bloom than annuals but require less care.

Many perennials benefit from being divided every few years, usually in early spring while the plants are still dormant or, in some cases, after flowering. Division keeps perennials vigorous and in some cases helps control their spread. Dig the plant up, remove dead debris, break the plant into several pieces using a sharp knife, spade or saw, and replant some or all of the pieces. Share extra pieces with family, friends and neighbors.

Trees & Shrubs

Trees and shrubs provide the bones of the garden. They are often the slowest growing plants but usually live the longest. Characterized by leaf type, they may be deciduous or evergreen, and needled or broad-leaved.

Trees should have as little disturbed soil as possible at the bottom of the planting hole. Loose dirt settles over time and sinking even an inch can kill some trees. The prepared area for trees and shrubs needs to be at least two to four times bigger than the rootball.

Staking is necessary only for trees over 5' tall. Stakes support the rootball until it grows enough to support the tree. Stakes should allow the trunk to move with the wind.

Pruning is more often required for shrubs than trees. It helps them maintain an attractive shape and can improve blooming. Consult a book such as *Tree & Shrub Gardening for Ohio.*

Training vines to climb arbors adds structure to the garden.

Lilies bloom throughout the summer.

Roses

Roses are beautiful shrubs with lovely, often fragrant blooms. Traditionally, most roses bloomed only once in the growing season, but new varieties bloom all, or almost all, summer. Repeat blooming (recurrent) roses should be deadheaded to encourage more flower production. One-time bloomers should be left for the colorful hips that develop.

Generally, roses prefer a fertile, well-prepared planting area. A guideline is to prepare an area 24" across, front to back and side to side, and 24" deep. Add plenty of compost or other fertile organic matter, although many roses are quite durable and adapt to poorer conditions. Grafted roses should be planted with the graft two inches below the soil line. Keep roses well watered during the growing season. To reduce the spread of blackspot, avoid getting water on the foliage.

Vines

Vines or climbing plants are useful for screening and shade, especially in a location too small for a tree. They may be woody or herbaceous and annual or perennial. Vines may physically cling to surfaces, may have wrapping tendrils or stems or may need to be tied in place with string.

Sturdy trellises, arbors, porch railings, fences, walls, poles and trees are all possible vine supports. If a support is needed, ensure it's in place before you plant to avoid disturbing the roots later. Choose a support that is suitable for the vine you are growing. It needs to be sturdy enough to hold the plant up and should match the growing habit—clinging, wrapping or tied—of the vine.

Bulbs, Corms & Tubers

These plants have fleshy underground storage organs that allow them to survive extended periods of dormancy. They are often grown for the bright splashes of color their flowers provide. They may flower in spring, summer or fall. Each has an ideal depth and time of year at which it should be planted.

Hardy bulbs can be left in the ground to flower year after year. Some popular tender plants are grown from bulbs, corms or tubers that are generally lifted from the garden in late summer or fall as the foliage dies back. They are stored in a

Herbs are practical and ornamental.

cool, frost-free location for winter, to be replanted in spring.

Herbs

Herbs are plants with medicinal, culinary or other economic purposes. A few common culinary herbs are included in this book. Even if you don't cook with them, the often-fragrant foliage adds its aroma to the garden, and the plants can be quite decorative in form, leaf and flower. A container of your favorite herbs—perhaps conveniently placed

Ornamental grasses add colour, variety and texture.

near the kitchen door—will yield plenty of flavor and fragrance all summer.

Many herbs have pollen-producing flowers that attract butterflies, bees, hummingbirds and predatory insects to your garden. Predatory insects feast on problem insects such as aphids, mealy bugs and whiteflies.

Foliage Plants

Many plants are grown primarily for their decorative foliage rather than their flowers, which may also be decorative. Many such plants are included in other sections of this book, but we have set aside a few for the unique touch their foliage adds to the garden.

Ornamental grasses and grass-like plants offer a variety of forms, textures and foliage colors and provide interest year-round when the withered blades are left to stand through winter. They are cut back in early spring, and are divided when the clumps begin to die out in the centers.

Ferns provide a lacy foliage accent and combine attractively with broad-leaved perennials and shrubs. Ferns are a common sight in moist and shady gardens, but some species survive in full sun. A bonus is that most ferns are not palatable to deer.

The other foliage plants in this section can be treated as the annuals, perennials or woody plants they are.

A Final Comment

The more you discover about the fascinating world of plants—whether it be from books, talking to other gardeners, appreciating the creative designs of others, or experimenting with something new in your own garden—the more rewarding your gardening experience will be. This book is intended as a guide to germinate and grow your passion for plants.

Ageratum
Ageratum

A. h. 'Hawaii Blue' (above), *A. houstonianum* (below)

The fluffy flowers of ageratum, often in shades of blue, add softness and texture to the garden.

Growing

Ageratum prefers **full sun** but tolerates partial shade. The soil should be **fertile, moist** and **well drained**. A moisture-retaining mulch prevents the soil from drying out excessively. Deadhead to prolong blooming and keep plants looking tidy.

Tips

Almost completely covered in flowers when in bloom, the small varieties make excellent edging plants for flowerbeds and are attractive when grouped in masses or grown in planters. The tall varieties can be included in the center of a flowerbed and are useful as cut flowers.

Also called: floss flower
Features: fuzzy flowers in blue, purple, pink or white; mounded habit **Height:** 6–36"
Spread: 6–18"

Recommended

A. houstonianum forms a large, leggy mound that can grow up to 24" tall. Many available cultivars have a low, bushy habit and grow about half as tall. Flowers are produced in shades of blue, purple, pink or white.

The genus name Ageratum is of Greek origin and means 'without age,' in reference to the long-lasting flowers.

Alyssum
Lobularia

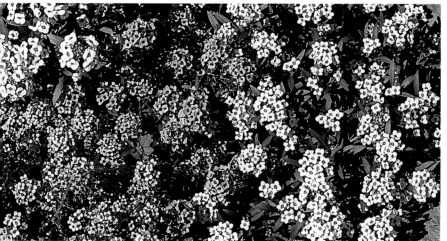

L. maritima (above & below)

Alyssum is excellent for creating soft edges. As a bonus, it self-seeds, popping up along pathways and between stones late in the season, giving summer a sweet sendoff.

Growing
Alyssum prefers **full sun** but tolerates light shade. **Well-drained** soil of **average fertility** is preferred, but poor soil is tolerated. Alyssum may die back a bit during the heat and humidity of summer. Trim the plants back and water periodically in summer to encourage new growth and more flowers when the weather cools.

Tips
Alyssum creeps around rock gardens, billows over rock walls and fills the edges of beds and containers. It can be seeded into cracks and crevices of walkways and between patio stones. Once established, it readily reseeds. It is also good for filling in spaces between taller plants in borders and mixed containers.

Recommended
L. maritima forms a low, spreading mound of foliage. The entire plant appears to be covered in tiny, fragrant blossoms when in full flower. Cultivars with flowers in a wide range of colors are available.

Leave alyssum plants in the garden over winter. In spring, remove the previous year's growth to expose the self-sown seedlings beneath.

Also called: sweet alyssum
Features: fragrant flowers in pink, purple, yellow, salmon or white **Height:** 3–12"
Spread: 6–24"

Angelonia
Angelonia

A. angustifolia 'Alba' (above), *A. a.* 'Blue Pacific' (below)

With its loose, airy spikes of orchid-like flowers, *Angelonia* makes a welcome addition to the garden.

Growing
Angelonia prefers **full sun** but tolerates a bit of shade. The soil should be **fertile, moist** and **well drained**. Although this plant grows naturally in damp areas, such as along ditches and near ponds, it is fairly drought tolerant. Plant out after the chance of frost has passed.

Tips
Angelonia makes a good addition to an annual or mixed border, where it is most attractive when planted in groups. It is also well suited to a pondside or streamside planting.

Recommended
*A. **angustifolia*** is a bushy, upright, tender subshrub with loose spikes of flowers in varied shades of purple. Cultivars with white or bicolored flowers are available.

The individual flowers look a bit like orchid blossoms, but Angelonia *is actually in the same family as snapdragon.*

Also called: angel wings, summer snapdragon
Features: attractive purple, blue, white or bicolored flowers **Height:** 12–24"
Spread: 12"

Bacopa
Sutera

S. *cordata* (above & below)

Bacopa is a perennial that is grown as an annual outdoors. It also thrives as a houseplant in a bright room.

Bacopa snuggles under and around the stems of taller plants, forming a dense carpet dotted with tiny, white to pale lavender flowers and eventually drifting over pot edges to form a waterfall of stars.

Growing

Bacopa grows well in **partial shade** with protection from the hot afternoon sun. The soil should be of **average fertility, humus rich, moist** and **well drained**.

Don't allow this plant to dry out, or the leaves will quickly die. Cutting back dead growth may encourage new shoots to form.

Tips

Bacopa is a popular plant for hanging baskets, mixed containers and window boxes. Because it fizzles quickly when the weather gets hot, particularly if you forget to water, it is not recommended as a bedding plant. Plant it where you will see it every day, so you will remember to water it.

Recommended

S. cordata is a compact, trailing plant that bears small, white flowers all summer. Cultivars with larger white or lavender flowers or variegated, gold-and-green foliage are available.

Features: decorative white or lavender flowers; attractive foliage; trailing habit **Height:** 3–6" **Spread:** 12–20"

Begonia
Begonia

*W*ant beautiful flowers, a compact or trailing habit and decorative foliage? There is sure to be a begonia to fulfill your shade-gardening needs.

Growing
Begonias prefer **light to partial shade** and **fertile, neutral to acidic, well-drained** soil **rich in organic matter**. Some wax begonias tolerate sun if their soil is kept moist. Allow the soil to dry out slightly between waterings, particularly for tuberous begonias. Plant begonias only once the soil has warmed. In cold soil, they may succumb to root rot or become stunted and fail to thrive.

Tips
All begonias are useful for shaded garden beds and planters. The trailing tuberous varieties can be used in hanging baskets and along rock walls, where the flowers will cascade over the edges. Wax begonias have a neat, rounded habit that makes them particularly attractive as edging plants. Rex begonias, with their dramatic foliage, are useful as specimen plants in containers and beds.

Recommended
B. **Rex Cultorum Hybrids** (rex begonias) are grown for their dramatic, colorful foliage.

B. semperflorens (wax begonias) have pink, white, red or bicolored flowers and green, bronze, reddish or white-variegated foliage.

B. semperflorens Cocktail Series (above)
B. x *tuberhybrida* (below)

B. x *tuberhybrida* (tuberous begonias) are generally sold as tubers. They are popular for their flowers, which come in many shades of red, pink, yellow, orange or white.

Features: pink, white, red, yellow, orange, bicolored or picotee flowers; decorative foliage
Height: 6–24" **Spread:** 6–24"

Black-Eyed Susan

Rudbeckia

R. h. 'Becky Mixed' (above), R. hirta (below)

lack-eyed Susan brightens up any spot in the garden, and its tolerance for heavy soils makes it useful in new developments, where the topsoil is often very thin.

Growing

Black-eyed Susan grows equally well in **full sun** or **light shade**. The soil should be of **average fertility, humus rich, moist** and **well drained**. This plant tolerates heavy clay soil or sandy soil and hot, dry weather. It blooms well even in the hottest part of the garden. Deadhead to prolong blooming. When growing in loose, moist soil, black-eyed Susan may reseed itself.

Tips

Plant black-eyed Susan individually or in groups, in beds and borders, large containers, meadow plantings and wildflower gardens.

Recommended

R. hirta forms a bristly mound of foliage and bears bright yellow, daisy-like flowers with brown centers from summer until the first fall frost. A wide variety of cultivars are available, including dwarf plants and plants with double flowers or flowers with lime green centers.

Perennial varieties are also available.

Black-eyed Susan is a long-lasting vase flower. It makes a stunning display when combined with purple and burgundy flowers.

Also called: gloriosa daisy, annual rudbeckia, coneflower **Features:** yellow, orange, red, mahogany, brown or bicolored flowers with brown or green centers **Height:** 8–36" or more **Spread:** 12–18"

Calendula
Calendula

Bright and charming, calendulas produce attractive warm-colored flowers in early summer and again in late summer and fall.

Growing
Calendula does equally well in **full sun** or **partial shade**. **Well-drained** soil of **average fertility** is preferred. Calendula likes cool weather and can withstand a moderate frost. Sow seed directly into the garden in mid-spring. Deadhead to prolong blooming and keep plants looking neat. If plants fade in summer heat, cut them back to 4–6" above the ground to promote new growth, or pull them up and seed new ones. Either method provides a good fall display.

C. o. 'Apricot Surprise' (above), C. officinalis (below)

Tips
This informal plant looks attractive in borders and mixed into the vegetable patch. It can also be used in mixed planters.

Recommended
C. officinalis is a vigorous, tough, upright plant that bears daisy-like, single or double flowers in a wide range of yellow and orange shades. Several cultivars are available.

Calendula is a cold-hardy annual that often continues flowering, even through a layer of snow, until the ground freezes completely.

Also called: pot marigold, English marigold
Features: cream, yellow, gold, orange or apricot flowers; long blooming period
Height: 10–24" **Spread:** 8–20"

California Poppy
Eschscholtzia

E. californica (above & below)

A mound of delicate, feathery, gray-green foliage topped with shimmering, satiny flowers in sorbet shades makes this annual a repeat favorite.

Growing

California poppy prefers **full sun**. The soil should be of **poor to average fertility** and **well drained**. In too fertile a soil, lush growth with few flowers occurs. Established plants tolerate drought. Sow seed directly into the garden in early spring for flowers in summer. Water seedlings regularly until flowering begins.

Tips

California poppy can be included in an annual border or annual planting in a cottage garden. This plant self-seeds wherever it is planted, coming back year after year, making it a great addition to a meadow or rock garden.

Recommended

E. californica forms a mound of delicate, feathery foliage. Satiny orange or yellow flowers are produced all summer. The many available cultivars include ones with double flowers or shades of red, cream or pink.

California poppy is not fond of sharing space with plants that steal the sun. Plant it in a sunny, open space, and it will thrive.

Features: orange, yellow, red, cream, pink flowers; mounding habit; feathery foliage
Height: 8–18" **Spread:** 8–18"

Fan Flower

Scaevola

Fan flower's intriguing one-sided flowers add interest to hanging baskets, planters and window boxes.

Growing

Fan flower grows well in **full sun** or **light shade**. The soil should be of **average fertility, moist** and very **well drained**. Water regularly, because this plant doesn't like to dry out completely, but it does recover quickly from wilting when watered.

Tips

Fan flower is popular for hanging baskets and containers, but it can also be used along the tops of rock walls and in rock gardens, where it will trail down. This plant makes an interesting addition to mixed borders, or it can be used under shrubs, where the long, trailing stems form an attractive groundcover.

Recommended

S. aemula forms a mound of foliage from which trailing stems emerge. The fan-shaped flowers come in shades of purple, usually with white bases. The many improved cultivars are much preferred over the species.

S. aemula (above & below)

Given the right conditions, this Australian plant flowers abundantly from April through to frost.

Features: unique flowers in blue or purple; trailing habit **Height:** up to 8"
Spread: up to 36" or more

Geranium
Pelargonium

P. peltatum Fireworks Series (above), *P. peltatum* (below)

Tough, predictable, sun-loving and drought-resistant, geraniums have earned their place as flowering favorites in the annual garden. If you are looking for something out of the ordinary, seek out the scented geraniums with their fragrant and often-decorative foliage.

Growing

Geraniums prefer **full sun** but tolerate partial shade, although they may not bloom as profusely. The soil should be **fertile** and **well drained**.

Deadheading is essential to keep geraniums blooming and looking neat.

Tips

Geraniums are very popular in borders, beds, planters, hanging baskets and window boxes.

Usually treated as annuals, geraniums are perennials that can be overwintered indoors in a bright room.

Recommended

P. peltatum (ivy-leaved geranium) has thick, waxy leaves and a trailing habit. Many cultivars are available.

P. **species** and **cultivars** (scented geraniums, scented pelargoniums) form a large group of geraniums that have scented leaves. The scents are grouped into the categories of rose, mint, citrus, fruit, spice and pungent.

P. zonale (zonal geranium) is a bushy plant with red, pink, purple, orange or white flowers and, frequently, banded or multicolored foliage. Many cultivars are available.

Features: red, pink, violet, orange, salmon, white or purple flowers; decorative or scented foliage; variable habits **Height:** 8–24" **Spread:** 6"–4'

Heliotrope
Heliotropium

Heliotrope's big clusters of fragrant flowers on bushy plants have renewed the popularity of this old-fashioned favorite.

Growing
Heliotrope grows best in **full sun**. The soil should be **fertile, rich in organic matter, moist** and **well drained**. Overwatering can kill heliotrope, but a plant left to dry to the point of wilting recovers slowly. This cold-sensitive plant should be set outside only after the danger of frost has passed. Cover heliotrope or bring it indoors if unseasonable frost is expected and before the first fall frost if you plan to overwinter it indoors.

Tips
Heliotrope is ideal for growing in containers or flowerbeds near windows and patios, where the wonderful fragrance of the flowers can be enjoyed. It can also be grown indoors in a bright, sunny window.

Recommended
H. arborescens is a low, bushy shrub that is treated as an annual. It produces large clusters of fragrant flowers in purple, blue or white. Many cultivars are available.

H. arborescens (above & below)

Heliotrope kept a little on the dry side tends to have more strongly scented flowers.

Also called: cherry pie plant
Features: fragrant flowers in purple, blue or white; attractive foliage **Height:** 18–24"
Spread: 12–24"

Impatiens
Impatiens

I. walleriana (above), *I. hawkeri* (below)

Impatiens are the high-wattage darlings of the shade garden, delivering masses of flowers in a wide variety of colors.

Growing

Impatiens do best in **partial shade** or **light shade** but tolerate full shade or, if kept moist, full sun. The soil should be **fertile, humus rich, moist** and **well drained**. New Guinea impatiens is the best adapted to sunny locations.

New impatiens varieties are introduced every year, expanding the selection of sizes, forms and colors available for our gardens.

Tips

Impatiens are known for their ability to grow and flower profusely even in shade. Mass plant them in beds under trees, along shady fences or walls or in porch planters. They also look lovely in hanging baskets. New Guinea impatiens is grown as much for its variegated leaves as for its flowers.

Recommended

I. hawkeri (New Guinea hybrids; New Guinea impatiens) flowers in shades of red, orange, pink, purple or white. The foliage is often variegated, with a yellow stripe down the center of each leaf.

I. walleriana (impatiens, busy Lizzie) flowers in shades of purple, red, burgundy, pink, yellow, salmon, orange, apricot and white and can be bicolored. Dozens of cultivars are available.

Features: purple, red, burgundy, pink, yellow, salmon, orange, apricot, white or bicolored flowers; flowers well in shade **Height:** 6–36" **Spread:** 12–24"

Love-in-a-Mist

Nigella

N. damascena (above & below)

*L*ove-in-a-mist's ferny foliage and delicate, blue flowers blend beautifully with most plants. With a tendency to self-sow, love-in-a-mist may show up in unexpected spots in your garden for years to come.

Growing
Love-in-a-mist prefers **full sun**. The soil should be of **average fertility, light** and **well drained**. Direct sow seeds at two-week intervals from spring to early June to prolong the blooming period. The seedlings of this self-seeding plant, which resent being disturbed, should be transplanted carefully, if at all.

Tips
An attractive, airy plant, love-in-a-mist is often used in mixed beds and borders. The unusual flowers appear to float above the delicate foliage. In hot weather, blooming may slow, and the plants may die back. Cut the plants back to rejuvenate them.

The stems of this plant can be a bit floppy. Poking some twiggy sticks into the dirt around the plant when it is young can offer support as it grows.

Recommended
N. damascena forms a loose mound of finely divided foliage. Cultivars are available in a wide variety of flower colors and forms, including bicolored and double-flowered varieties.

Also called: devil-in-a-bush
Features: exotic flowers in blue, white, pink or purple; feathery foliage; interesting seed pods **Height:** 16–24" **Spread:** 8–12"

Marigold
Tagetes

T. patula Boy Series (above), *T. patula* cultivar (below)

From the large, exotic, ruffled flowers of African marigold to the tiny flowers on the low-growing signet marigold, the warm colors and fresh scent of marigolds add a festive touch to the garden.

Studies show that marigold's natural oils suppress nematodes, but it is debatable and doubtful whether marigolds deter insects and rabbits from devouring nearby plants.

Growing

Marigolds grow best in **full sun**. The soil should be of **average fertility** and **well drained**. These drought-tolerant plants also hold up well in windy, rainy weather. Sow seed directly or start early and transplant seedlings into the garden after the chance of frost has passed. Deadhead to prolong blooming and to keep plants tidy.

Tips

Mass planted or mixed with other plants, marigolds make a vibrant addition to beds, borders and container gardens. Marigolds thrive in the hottest, driest parts of your garden.

Recommended

Many cultivars are available.

T. erecta (African marigold, American marigold, Aztec marigold) produces the largest plants and the biggest flowers.

T. patula (French marigold) is low growing and offers a wide range of flower colors.

T. tenuifolia (signet marigold) has recently become more popular because of its feathery foliage and small, dainty flowers.

T. triploid hybrids (triploid marigold), developed by crossing French and African marigolds, combine large flowers and compact growth.

Features: brightly colored yellow, red, orange, brown, gold, cream or bicolored flowers; fragrant foliage **Height:** 6–36" **Spread:** 12–24"

Million Bells

Calibrachoa

'Terracotta' (above), 'Trailing Pink' (below)

*M*illion bells is charming, and, given the right conditions, it blooms continually during the growing season.

Growing
Million bells prefers **full sun**. The soil should be **fertile, moist** and **well drained**. Although it prefers to be watered regularly, million bells is fairly drought resistant once established.

Tips
Popular for planters and hanging baskets, million bells is also attractive in beds and borders. It grows all summer and needs plenty of room to spread or it will overtake other flowers. Pinch the plants back to keep them compact.

Also called: trailing petunia **Features:** pink, purple, yellow, red-orange, white or blue flowers; trailing habit **Height:** 6–12" **Spread:** up to 24"

Recommended
C. **hybrids** have dense, trailing habits. Their small flowers look like petunias, and cultivars are available in a wide range of flower colors.

Million bells blooms well into fall. It becomes hardier over summer and as the weather cools.

Moss Rose
Portulaca

For a brilliant show in the hottest, driest, most sun-baked and neglected area of the garden, you can't go wrong with moss rose.

Growing

Moss rose requires **full sun**. The soil should be of **poor fertility, sandy** and **well drained**. If you sow directly outdoors, rain may transport the tiny seeds to unexpected places. To ensure that you have plants where you want them, start seed indoors. Moss rose also self-seeds.

Tips

Moss rose is ideal for garden spots that don't get much water, such as under the eaves of a house or in dry, rocky, exposed areas along pathways and in rock walls. It is also great for people who like hanging baskets but sometimes neglect to water them.

Recommended

P. grandiflora forms a bushy mound of succulent foliage. It bears delicate, silky, rose-like, single or double flowers profusely all summer. Many cultivars are available, including ones with flowers that stay open on cloudy days.

P. grandiflora (above & below)

Low-maintenance moss rose plants can be placed close together and allowed to intertwine for an interesting and attractive effect.

Also called: purslane **Features:** drought- and heat-resistant flowers in red, pink, yellow, white, purple, orange or peach **Height:** 4–12" **Spread:** 6–12" or more

Nasturtium
Tropaeolum

Easy to grow, fast growing and bearing brightly colored flowers, nasturtium is popular with beginners and experienced gardeners alike.

Growing
Nasturtium prefers **full sun** but tolerates some shade. The soil should be of **poor to average fertility, light, moist** and **well drained**. Soil that is too rich or has too much nitrogen fertilizer results in a lot of leaves but very few flowers. Let the soil drain completely between waterings. Sow directly in the garden once the danger of frost has passed.

Tips
Nasturtium is used in beds, borders, containers and hanging baskets and on sloped banks. The climbing varieties are grown up trellises or over rock walls or places that need concealing. Nasturtium thrives in poor locations, and it make an interesting addition to plantings on hard-to-mow slopes.

Recommended
T. majus has a trailing habit, but many of the cultivars have bushier, more refined habits and offer differing flower colors or variegated foliage.

T. majus (above), *T. m.* 'Alaska' (below)

The edible leaves and flowers of nasturtium add a peppery flavor to salads.

Features: brightly colored red, orange, yellow, burgundy, pink, cream, gold, white or bicolored, edible flowers; attractive, edible leaves; varied habits **Height:** 12–18" for dwarf varieties; up to 10' for trailing varieties
Spread: equal to height

Petunia
Petunia

Milliflora type 'Fantasy' (above), Multiflora type (below)

For speedy growth, prolific blooming, ease of care and a huge number of varieties, petunias are hard to beat.

Growing

Petunias prefer **full sun**. The soil should be of **average to rich fertility, light, sandy** and **well drained**. Pinch the plants halfway back in mid-summer to keep them bushy and to encourage new growth and flowers.

Tips

Use petunias in beds, borders, containers and hanging baskets.

Recommended

P. x *hybrida* is a large group of popular, sun-loving annuals that fall into three categories. **Grandifloras** have the largest (but fewest) flowers in the widest range of colors, but they can be damaged by rain

Millifloras have the smallest flowers in the narrowest range of colors, but this type is the most prolific and least likely to be damaged by heavy rain. **Multifloras** bear intermediate sizes and numbers of flowers and suffer intermediate rain damage. Cultivars of all types are available, and new varieties are released almost every year.

The rekindled interest in petunias resulted largely from the development of exciting new varieties, such as the multiflora Wave Series petunias. These vigorously spreading, dense-growing hybrids tolerate wet weather and offer tremendous options for hanging baskets, containers and borders.

Features: pink, purple, red, white, yellow, coral, blue or bicolored flowers; versatility
Height: 6–18" **Spread:** 12–24" or more

Poppy
Papaver

Poppies look like they were meant to grow in groups, Swaying in a breeze atop often-curving stems, the flowers seem to be engaged in lively conversations.

Growing
Poppies grow best in **full sun**. The soil should be **fertile** and **sandy** with a lot of **organic matter** mixed in. **Good drainage** is essential. Direct sow every two weeks in spring, or sow in fall for earlier spring blooms. Mix the tiny seeds with fine sand for even sowing. Do not cover, because the seeds need light for germination. Deadhead to prolong blooming.

Tips
Poppies work well in mixed borders. They fill empty spaces early in the season, then die back over summer, leaving room for slower plants to fill in. Poppies can also be used in rock gardens. As cut flowers, poppies look good in fresh arrangements.

Recommended
P. nudicaule (Icelandic poppy) bears red, orange, yellow, pink or white flowers in spring and early summer.

P. orientale (Oriental poppy) is a perennial that is sometimes mistaken for an annual when it dies back over summer. Oriental poppy is renowned for its large, bright red, dark-centered early-summer flowers.

P. rhoeas (Flanders poppy, field poppy, corn poppy) forms a basal rosette of foliage above which rise the long-stemmed flowers in a wide range of colors.

Features: brightly colored red, pink, white, purple, yellow or orange flowers
Height: 24–36" **Spread:** 12"

P. orientale (above), *P. nudicaule* (below)

Be careful when weeding around faded summer plants so that you don't weed out late-summer poppy seedlings, which may flower in fall or the following spring (as biennials).

Sage
Salvia

S. *splendens* (red) and S. *farinacea* (purple) with purple lobelia (above), S. *viridis* (below)

The tender, annual salvias should be part of every garden. The attractive and varied forms have something to offer any garden style.

Growing

Salvias prefer **full sun** but tolerate light shade. The soil should be **moist, well drained** and of **average to rich fertility,** with a lot of **organic matter.**

Tips

Salvias look good grouped in beds or borders and in containers. The long-lasting flowers are good in cut-flower arrangements.

To keep the plants producing flowers, water often and fertilize monthly.

Recommended

S. *argentea* (silver sage), actually a biennial, is grown for its large, fuzzy, silvery leaves.

S. *coccinea* (Texas sage) is a bushy, upright plant that bears whorled spikes of white, pink, blue or purple flowers.

S. *farinacea* (mealy cup sage, blue sage) has bright blue flowers clustered along stems powdered with silver. Cultivars are available.

S. *splendens* (salvia, scarlet sage) is grown for its spikes of bright red, tubular flowers. Cultivars are now available in white, pink, purple and orange.

S. *viridis* (S. *horminium;* annual clary sage) is grown for its colorful pink, purple, blue or white bracts, not its flowers.

Features: red, blue, purple, burgundy, pink, orange, salmon, yellow, cream, white or bicolored flowers; attractive foliage
Height: 8"–4' **Spread:** 8"–4'

Snapdragon
Antirrhinum

Snapdragon is among the most appealing plants. The flower colors are always rich and vibrant, and even the most jaded gardeners are tempted to squeeze open the dragons' mouths.

Growing
Snapdragon prefers **full sun** but tolerates light or partial shade. The soil should be **fertile, rich in organic matter** and **well drained**. This plant prefers a **neutral to alkaline** soil; it does not perform as well in acidic soil. Do not cover seeds when sowing, because they require light for germination.

To encourage bushy growth, pinch the tips of the young plants. To promote further blooming and to prevent the plant from dying back before the end of the season, cut off the flower spikes as they fade.

Tips
The shortest snapdragon varieties work well near the front of a border, and the tallest ones look good in the center or back. The dwarf and medium-height varieties can also be used in planters. A trailing variety does well in hanging baskets.

Recommended
A. majus has many available cultivars. They are generally grouped into three size categories: dwarf, medium and giant.

A. *majus* cultivars (above & below)

Snapdragons are beautiful and long-lasting in fresh flower arrangements. The buds continue to mature and open even after the spike is cut from the plant.

Features: attractive and entertaining flowers in white, cream, yellow, orange, red, maroon, pink, purple or bicolored **Height:** 6"–4'
Spread: 6–24"

Sunflower

Helianthus

H. a. 'Teddy Bear' (above), *H. annuus* cultivar (below)

Each of the many sunflower options adds cheerful charm to any garden. We have never seen a sunflower we didn't like.

Growing

Sunflower grows best in **full sun**. The soil should be of **average fertility, humus rich, moist** and **well drained**. Successive sowings from spring to early summer prolong the blooming period.

The annual sunflower is an excellent flower for a child's garden. The seeds are big and easy to handle, and they germinate quickly. Until the flower finally appears on top, the plants grow continually upward, and their progress can be measured.

Tips

Low-growing varieties can be used in beds, borders and containers. Tall varieties work well at the back of borders and make good screens and temporary hedges. The tallest varieties may need staking.

Recommended

H. annuus (common sunflower) has attractive cultivars in a wide range of heights, with single stems or branching habits. The flowers come in a variety of colors, in single to fully double forms.

Features: late-summer flowers, most commonly yellow, but also orange, red, brown, cream or bicolored, typically with brown, purple or rusty red centers; edible seeds **Height:** 16" for dwarf varieties; up to 15' for giants **Spread:** 12–24"

Verbena

Verbena

V. bonariensis (above), *V.* x *hybrida* (below)

Verbenas offer butterflies a banquet. Butterfly visitors include tiger swallowtails, silver-spotted skippers, great spangled fritillaries and painted ladies.

Growing

Verbenas grow best in **full sun**. The soil should be **fertile** and very **well drained**. Pinch back young plants for bushy growth.

Tips

Use verbenas on rock walls and in beds, borders, rock gardens, containers, hanging baskets and window boxes. They make good substitutes for ivy-leaved geranium where the sun is hot and where a roof overhang keeps the mildew-prone verbenas dry.

Features: red, pink, purple, blue, yellow, scarlet, silver, peach or white flowers, some with white centers **Height:** 8"–5'
Spread: 12–36"

Recommended

V. bonariensis is a tender perennial that is often treated as an annual. It forms a low clump of foliage from which tall, stiff stems bear clusters of small, purple flowers.

V. x *hybrida* (garden verbena) is a bushy plant that may be upright or spreading. It bears clusters of small flowers in a wide range of colors. Cultivars are available.

The Romans, it is said, believed verbena could rekindle the flames of dying love. They named it herba Veneris or 'plant of Venus.'

Viola
Viola

V. x wittrockiana (above), V. tricolor (below)

Sow seed indoors in early winter for spring flowers and sow in mid-summer for fall and early-winter blooms. Seeds germinate best when kept in darkness until they sprout.

Violas are a cottage garden staple. Often self-seeding, they pop up in unexpected places such as gravel driveways, between evergreen shrubs and in the cracks of a sidewalk.

Growing
Violas prefer **full sun** but tolerate partial shade. The soil should be **fertile, moist** and **well drained**. Violas perform best when the weather is cool, and they may die back completely during hot summer weather. The plants may rejuvenate in fall, but it is often easier to plant new ones once the weather cools. An early fall planting of violas will provide color until the first hard frost.

Tips
Violas can be used in beds, borders and containers, and they look great mixed in with spring-flowering bulbs.

Recommended
V. tricolor (Johnny-jump-up) are small, bushy plants that bear small, multicolored flowers of purple, white and yellow. Some varieties have flowers in a single color, usually purple.

V. x wittrockiana (pansy) bears flowers in blue, purple, red, orange, yellow, pink or white, often multicolored or with face-like markings. Many cultivars are available.

Features: blue, purple, red, orange, yellow, pink, white or multicolored flowers; best in cool spring and fall weather **Height:** 3–10" **Spread:** 6–12"

Aster

Aster

Among the final plants to bloom before the snow flies, asters have typically purple or pink flowers that contrast with the yellow-flowered perennials common in the late-summer and fall garden.

Growing

Asters prefer **full sun** but tolerate partial shade. The soil should be **fertile, moist** and **well drained**. Pinch or shear these plants back in early summer to promote dense growth and reduce disease problems. Mulch in winter to protect the plants from temperature fluctuations. Divide every two to three years to maintain vigor and control spread.

Tips

Use asters in the middle of borders and in cottage gardens, or naturalize them in wild gardens. You may need to protect your plants from munching visitors, because they are a favorite food of deer and rabbits.

Recommended

Some aster species have recently been reclassified under the genus *Symphyotrichum*. You may see both names at garden centers.

A. novae-angliae (Michaelmas daisy, New England aster) is an upright, spreading, clump-forming perennial that bears yellow-centered, purple flowers. Many cultivars are available.

A. novae-angliae (above), *A. novi-belgii* (below)

A. novi-belgii (Michaelmas daisy, New York aster) is a dense, upright, clump-forming perennial with purple flowers. Many cultivars are available.

Features: late-summer to mid-fall flowers in red, white, blue, purple or pink, often with yellow centers **Height:** 10"–5' **Spread:** 18–36" **Hardiness:** zones 3–8

Astilbe

Astilbe

A. x arendsii cultivars (above), *A. x arendsii* 'Bressingham Beauty' (below)

Astilbes are beacons in the shade. Their high-impact flowers will brighten any gloomy section of your garden.

Growing

Astilbes grow best in **light or partial shade** in soil that is **fertile, humus rich, acidic, moist** and **well drained**. Heavy shade reduces flowering. Although astilbes appreciate moist soil, they don't like standing water.

Astilbes should be divided every three years or so to maintain plant vigor. Root masses may lift out of the soil as the plants mature. Add a layer of topsoil and mulch if lifting occurs.

Tips

Astilbes can be grown near the edges of bog gardens and ponds, in woodland gardens and in moist shaded borders.

Recommended

Many species, hybrids and cultivars of astilbes are available. In general these plants form bushy clumps of leaves and bear plumes of colorful flowers. The following are a few popular selections.

*A. x **arendsii*** is a group of hybrids with many available cultivars. **'Avalanche'** bears white flowers. **'Bressingham Beauty'** has pink flowers. **'Fanal'** produces red flowers.

*A. **chinensis** var. **pumila*** is a dense, vigorous low-growing, spreading perennial that tolerates dry soil better than other astilbe species.

*A. **japonica*** is a compact, clump-forming perennial. Its many cultivars are preferred over the rarely grown species. **'Deutschland'** has white flowers. **'Peach Blossom'** bears peachy pink flowers.

Features: summer flowers in white, pink, purple, peach or red; attractive foliage
Height: 10"–4' **Spread:** 8–36"
Hardiness: zones 3–9

Baptisia

Baptisia

B. australis (above & below)

Spikes of bright blue flowers in early summer and attractive green foliage make baptisia a worthy garden addition, even if it does take up a sizeable amount of real estate.

Growing

Baptisia prefers **full sun** and tolerates partial shade, but too much shade results in lank growth that flops over easily. The soil should be of **poor to average fertility, sandy** and **well drained** for this native prairie plant.

Tips

Baptisia can be used in an informal border or cottage-type garden. It is an attractive addition for a naturalized planting, on a slope or in any sunny, well-drained spot.

Recommended

B. australis is an upright or somewhat spreading, clump-forming plant that bears spikes of purple-blue flowers in early summer.

If you've had difficulties growing lupines, try the far less demanding baptisia instead.

Also called: false indigo **Features:** late-spring and early-summer flowers in purple-blue; bushy habit; delicate foliage **Height:** 3–5' **Spread:** 2–4' **Hardiness:** zones 3–9

Blazing Star
Liatris

Blazing star is an outstanding, long-lasting cut flower with fuzzy, spiked blossoms that rise above grass-like foliage and bloom from the top down.

Growing
Blazing star prefers **full sun**. The soil should be of **average fertility, sandy** and **humus rich**. Water well during the growing season but don't allow the plant to stand in water during cool weather. Mulch during summer to prevent moisture loss.

Trim off the spent flower spikes to promote a longer blooming period and to keep blazing star looking tidy. Divide every three or four years in fall. The clump will appear crowded when it is time to divide.

Tips
Use this native plant in borders and meadow plantings. Plant it in a location that has good drainage to avoid root rot in winter. Blazing star also grows well in planters.

Recommended
L. spicata is a clump-forming, erect plant. The flowers are pinkish purple or white. Several cultivars are available.

L. s. 'Kobold' (above), L. spicata (below)

Blazing star is a bee and butterfly magnet.

Also called: spike gayfeather, gayfeather
Features: summer flowers in purple or white; grass-like foliage **Height:** 18–36"
Spread: 18–24" **Hardiness:** zones 3–9

Bleeding Heart
Dicentra

E very garden should have a bleeding heart. Tucked away in a shady spot, this lovely plant appears in spring and fills the garden with fresh promise.

Growing
Bleeding hearts prefer **light shade** but tolerate partial or full shade. The soil should be **humus rich, moist** and **well drained**. Regular watering will keep the flowers coming until mid-summer. Very dry summer conditions cause the plants to die back, although they will revive in fall or the following spring, depending on the species. *D. eximia* and *D. spectabilis* rarely need dividing. *D. formosa* can be divided every three years or so.

Tips
Bleeding hearts can be naturalized in a woodland garden or grown in a border or rock garden. They make excellent early-season specimen plants and do well near ponds or streams.

D. formosa (above), *D. spectabilis* (below)

Recommended
*D. **eximia*** (fringed bleeding heart) forms a loose, mounded clump of lacy, fern-like foliage and bears pink or white flowers in spring and sporadically over summer.

*D. **formosa*** (western bleeding heart) is a low-growing, wide-spreading plant with pink flowers that fade to white as they mature. The most drought tolerant of the bleeding hearts, this species is the most likely to continue flowering all summer.

*D. **spectabilis*** (common bleeding heart, Japanese bleeding heart) forms a large, elegant mound that bears flowers with white inner petals and pink outer petals. Be prepared for it to enter dormancy by early July. Several cultivars are available.

All bleeding hearts contain toxic alkaloids, and some people develop allergic skin reactions from contact with these plants.

Features: spring and summer flowers of pink, white, red or purple; attractive foliage
Height: 1–4' **Spread:** 12–36"
Hardiness: zones 3–9

Butterfly Weed
Asclepias

A. *incarnata* (above), A. *tuberosa* (below)

Tender and annual species of Asclepias *are also available. Two common popular ones are* A. curassavica *(blood flower), with red, orange or yellow flowers, and* A. physocarpa *(swan plant), which produces whitish or greenish blooms.*

Native to North America, butter-fly weeds attract butterflies, most notably the monarch butterfly, for which they are a major food source.

Growing
Butterfly weeds grow best in **full sun.** The soil should be **fertile, moist** and **well drained,** although A. *tuberosa* is drought tolerant. To propagate, the seedlings can be transplanted as needed, but mature plants resent being divided.

Deadhead to encourage a second flush of blooms.

Tips
Use A. *tuberosa* in meadow plant-ings and borders, on dry banks, in neglected areas and in wildflower, cottage-style and butterfly gardens. Use A. *incarnata* in moist borders and in bog, pondside or streamside plantings.

Recommended
A. *incarnata* (swamp milkweed) forms a dense clump of thick stems that bear clusters of pink, white or light purple flowers in late spring or early summer. Cultivars are available.

A. *tuberosa* (butterfly weed) forms a clump of upright, leafy stems. It bears clusters of orange flowers from mid-summer to early fall. Cultivars are available.

Also called: milkweed, pleurisy root
Features: late-spring, summer and early-fall flowers in red, yellow, orange, white, pink or light purple; attracts butterflies.
Height: 18–36" **Spread:** 12–24"
Hardiness: zones 4–9

Campanula
Campanula

Thanks to their wide range of heights and habits, campanulas can be used almost anywhere in the garden.

Growing

Campanulas grow well in **full sun, partial shade** or **light shade.** The soil should be of **average to high fertility** and **well drained.** Mulch to keep the roots cool and moist in summer and protected in winter, particularly if snow cover is inconsistent. Deadhead to prolong blooming.

Tips

Plant upright and mounding campanulas in borders and in cottage gardens. Use low, spreading and trailing campanulas in rock gardens and on rock walls. You can also edge beds with the low-growing varieties.

Recommended

C. x **'Birch Hybrid'** is a low-growing, spreading plant. It bears light blue to mauve flowers in summer.

C. carpatica (Carpathian bellflower, Carpathian harebell) is a spreading, mounding perennial that bears blue, white or purple flowers in summer. Several cultivars are available.

C. glomerata (clustered bellflower) forms a clump of upright stems and bears clusters of purple, blue or white flowers throughout most of summer.

C. persicifolia (peach-leaved bellflower) is an upright perennial that bears white, blue or purple flowers from early to mid-summer.

C. persicifolia (above), C. carpatica 'White Clips' (below)

C. poscharskyana (Serbian bellflower) is a trailing perennial that likes to wind its way around other plants. It bears light violet blue flowers in summer and early fall.

Also called: bellflower **Features:** spring, summer and fall flowers of blue, white, purple or pink; varied growing habits **Height:** 4"–6' **Spread:** 12–36" **Hardiness:** zones 3–7

Chrysanthemum

Chrysanthemum

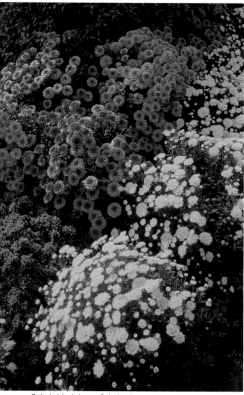

C. hybrids (above & below)

Chrysanthemum comes from Greek and means 'golden flower,' but these plants bloom in a wide range of bright colors.

Perk up your fall garden with a bright display of fall 'mums' with their masses of colorful flowers.

Growing

Chrysanthemums grow best in **full sun**. The soil should be **fertile, moist** and **well drained**. Plant as early in the growing season as possible to increase the chance that chrysanthemums will survive winter. Pinch the plants back in early summer to encourage bushy growth and increase flower production. Divide the plants every two or three years to keep them growing vigorously.

Tips

Chrysanthemums provide a blaze of fall color that lasts right until the first hard frost. In groups, or as specimen plants, they can be included in borders, in planters or in plantings close to the house. Plants purchased in fall can be added to spots where summer annuals have faded.

Recommended

C. **hybrids** form a diverse group of plants. One popular hybrid is *C.* **'Mei-Kyo,'** a vigorous grower that produces deep pink flowers in mid- to late October. The *C.* **'Prophet'** series, also popular, has cultivars with flowers in a wide range of colors, including **'Christine,'** with deep salmon pink flowers, and **'Raquel,'** with bright red flowers.

Features: late-summer and fall flowers in shades of orange, red, yellow, pink, red or purple; dense, bushy habit **Height:** 12–36" **Spread:** 2–4' **Hardiness:** zones 5–9

Columbine

Aquilegia

Delicate and beautiful, columbines add a touch of simple elegance to any garden. Blooming from spring through mid-summer, the long-lasting flowers herald the passing of cool spring weather and the arrival of summer.

Growing

Columbines grow well in **light or partial shade**. They prefer soil that is **fertile, moist** and **well drained,** but they adapt to most soil conditions. Division, although not required, can be done to propagate desirable plants. Because columbines dislike having their roots disturbed, divided plants may take a while to recover.

Tips

Use columbines in rock gardens, formal or casual borders and naturalized or woodland gardens. Plant them where other plants will hide their fading foliage as they die back over summer.

If leaf miners are a problem, cut the foliage back once flowering is complete and allow new foliage to fill in.

Recommended

A. canadensis (wild columbine, Canada columbine) is a native plant that is common in woodlands and fields. It bears yellow flowers with red spurs.

A. x *hybrida* (*A.* x *cultorum;* hybrid columbine) forms mounds of delicate foliage and has exceptional, showy flowers in a wide range of colors. Many selections are available.

A. canadensis (above)
A. x hybrida 'McKana Giants' (below)

A. vulgaris (European columbine, common columbine) has been used to develop many hybrids and cultivars with flowers in a variety of colors and forms, including double-flowered cultivars that look like frilly dahlias.

Features: spring and summer flowers in red, yellow, pink, purple, blue or white, often with petals and spurs of different colors; attractive foliage **Height:** 18–36" **Spread:** 12–24" **Hardiness:** zones 3–8

Coreopsis

Coreopsis

C. *auriculata* 'Nana' (above), C. *verticillata* (below)

These plants are easy to grow. They produce flowers all summer and make a fabulous addition to any garden.

Growing

Coreopsis plants grow best in **full sun**. The soil should be of **average fertility, sandy, light**, and **well drained**. Moist, cool locations with heavy soil can promote crown rot. Too fertile a soil encourages floppy growth. Deadhead the plants to keep them blooming.

Tips

Versatile coreopsis plants are useful in formal or informal borders and in meadow plantings and cottage gardens. They look best when planted in groups.

Recommended

C. auriculata 'Nana' (mouse-eared tickseed) is a low-growing species, well suited to rock gardens and the fronts of borders. It grows about 12" tall and spreads indefinitely, although slowly. It bears yellow-orange flowers in late spring.

C. verticillata (thread-leaf coreopsis) is a mound-forming plant with attractive, finely divided foliage and bright yellow flowers. It grows 24–32" tall and spreads 18". Available cultivars include **'Moonbeam,'** which forms a mound of delicate, lacy foliage and bears creamy yellow flowers.

Also called: tickseed **Features:** yellow, creamy yellow or yellow-orange flowers in late spring or summer; attractive foliage
Height: 12–32" **Spread:** 12–24"
Hardiness: zones 3–9

Daylily
Hemerocallis

Adaptability and durability combined with a variety of colors, blooming periods, sizes and textures explain the daylily's popularity.

Growing

Although daylilies grow in any light from **full sun to full shade**, shady locations yield fewer flowers. The soil should be **fertile, moist** and **well drained,** but these plants adapt to most conditions and are hard to kill once established. Divide every two to three years to keep the plants vigorous and to propagate them. They can, however, be left indefinitely without dividing.

Tips

Plant daylilies alone, or group them in borders, on banks and in ditches to control erosion. They can be naturalized in woodland or meadow gardens. Small varieties are nice in planters.

Deadhead to prolong the blooming period. Be careful when deadheading purple-flowered daylilies, because the sap can stain fingers and clothes.

'Dewey Roquemore' (above), 'Bonanza' (below)

Recommended

Daylilies species, cultivars and hybrids come in an almost infinite number of forms, sizes and colors. See your local garden center or daylily grower to find out what's available and what is most suitable for your garden.

Features: spring and summer flowers in any color except blue or pure white; grass-like foliage Height: 1–4' Spread: 1–4' Hardiness: zones 2–8

Foamflower

Tiarella

T. cordifolia (above & below)

With attractive leaves and delicate, starry, white flowers, foamflowers form handsome groundcovers in shaded areas.

Growing

Foamflowers prefer **partial, light or full shade without afternoon sun**. The ideal soil is **humus rich, moist** and **slightly**

Foamflowers propagate by underground stems that are easily pulled up to stop excessive spread.

acidic, but these plants adapt to most soils. Divide in spring. Deadhead to encourage reblooming. If the foliage fades or rusts in summer, remove the affected foliage to allow new growth to emerge.

Tips

Foamflowers are excellent groundcovers for shaded and woodland gardens. They can be included in shaded borders and left to naturalize in wild gardens.

Recommended

T. cordifolia is a low-growing, spreading plant that bears spikes of foamy-looking, white flowers. Cultivars are available.

T. 'Maple Leaf' is a clump-forming hybrid with bronze-green, maple-like leaves and pink-flushed flowers.

Features: spring and sometimes early-summer flowers in white or pink; decorative foliage
Height: 4–12" **Spread:** 12–24"
Hardiness: zones 3–8

Goat's Beard

Aruncus

Despite their imposing size, goat's beards have a soft and delicate appearance that results from the divided foliage and large, plumy, creamy white flowers.

Growing

These plants prefer **partial to full shade,** but in deep shade they bear fewer blooms. The soil should be **fertile, moist** and **humus rich.** Goat's beards tolerate full sun in the morning and early afternoon as long as the soil is kept evenly moist, but protect them from the afternoon sun. Divide in spring or fall. Use a sharp knife or an axe to cut the dense root mass into pieces. Fortunately, these plants rarely need dividing.

Tips

Goat's beards look very natural growing near the partly sunny edge of a woodland garden, in a native plant garden or in a large island planting. They may also be used in a border or alongside a stream or pond.

Recommended

A. aethusifolius (dwarf Korean goat's beard) forms a low-growing, compact mound and bears branched spikes of loosely held, creamy white flowers.

A. dioicus (giant goat's beard, common goat's beard) forms a large, bushy, shrub-like perennial with large plumes of creamy white flowers. Several cultivars are available.

A. dioicus (above & below)

Male and female flowers are produced on separate plants. In general, male flowers are full and fuzzy, whereas female flowers are more pendulous, but it can be difficult to distinguish them.

Features: early to mid-summer blooms in creamy white; shrub-like habit; attractive foliage and seedheads **Height:** 6"–6' **Spread:** 1–6' **Hardiness:** zones 3–8

Hardy Geranium
Geranium

G. sanguineum var. *striatum* (above)
G. sanguineum (below)

There is a type of geranium that suits every garden, thanks to the beauty and diversity of this hardy plant.

Growing
Hardy geraniums grow well in **full sun, partial shade** or **light shade**. They prefer soil of **average fertility** and **good**

If the foliage of a hardy geranium looks tatty in late summer, prune it back to rejuvenate the plant.

drainage. These plants dislike hot weather. *G. renardii* prefers a poor, well-drained soil. Divide in spring.

Tips
These long-flowering plants are great in a border; they fill in the spaces between shrubs and other larger plants, and they keep the weeds down. Hardy geraniums can be included in rock gardens and woodland gardens or mass planted as groundcovers.

Recommended
G. **'Brookside'** is a clump-forming, drought-tolerant plant with finely cut leaves and deep blue to violet blue flowers.

G. **macrorrhizum** (bigroot geranium, scented cranesbill) forms a spreading mound of fragrant foliage and bears flowers in various shades of pink. Cultivars are available.

G. **renardii** (Renard's geranium) forms a clump of deeply veined, crinkled, velvety foliage. A few white flowers with purple veins appear over summer, but the foliage remains the main attraction.

G. **sanguineum** (bloodred cranesbill, bloody cranesbill) forms a dense, mounding clump and bears bright magenta flowers. Many cultivars are available.

Also called: cranesbill geranium
Features: spring and summer flowers in white, red, pink, purple or blue; attractive, possibly fragrant foliage **Height:** 4–36"
Spread: 12–36" **Hardiness:** zones 3–8

Hosta

Hosta

reeders are always looking for new variations in hosta foliage. Swirls, stripes, puckers and ribs enhance the various leaf sizes, shapes and colors.

Growing

Hostas prefer **light or partial shade** but will grow in full shade. The soil should ideally be **fertile, moist** and **well drained,** but most soils are tolerated. Morning sun is preferable to afternoon sun in partial shade situations. Hostas are fairly drought tolerant, especially if given a mulch to help retain moisture. Division is not required but can be done every few years in spring or summer to propagate new plants.

Tips

Hostas are wonderful in woodland gardens and look very attractive when combined with ferns and other fine-textured plants. They are also good for mixed borders, particularly for hiding the ugly, leggy lower stems and branches of some shrubs. The dense growth and thick, shade-providing leaves of hostas help to suppress weeds.

Recommended

Hosta cultivars number in the hundreds, thanks to extensive crossbreeding and hybridizing. Visit your local garden center or get a mail-order catalogue to check availability.

H. fortunei 'Francee' (above)

If you like the foliage of hostas but not the flowers, you can remove the flower stems when they first emerge without harming the plant.

Also called: plantain lily
Features: decorative foliage; summer and fall flowers in white or purple **Height:** 4–36"
Spread: 6"–6' **Hardiness:** zones 3–8

Iris

Iris

I. sibirica (above), *I. germanica* 'Stepping Out' (below)

Irises are steeped in history and lore. Many people compare the available flower colors of bearded irises to a rainbow.

Growing

Irises prefer **full sun** but tolerate very light or dappled shade. The soil should be of **average fertility** and **well drained**. Japanese iris and Siberian iris prefer a moist but still well-drained soil.

Divide in late summer or early fall. Deadhead irises to keep them tidy. Cut back the foliage of Siberian iris in early spring.

Tips

All irises are popular as border plants, but Japanese iris and Siberian iris are also useful alongside streams or ponds. Dwarf cultivars make attractive additions to rock gardens

Even the residues left on your hands by handling irises may cause severe internal irritation if ingested, so wash your hands afterward. Do not plant irises close to children's play areas.

Recommended

Iris species and hybrids offer many selections. Among the most popular is the bearded iris, often a hybrid of **I. germanica**. It has the widest range of flower colors but is susceptible to possibly fatal attack by the iris borer. Non-susceptible irises include **I. ensata** (Japanese iris) and **I. sibirica** (Siberian iris). Check with your local garden center to determine availability.

Features: spring, summer and sometimes fall flowers in many shades of pink, red, purple, blue, white, brown or yellow; attractive foliage **Height:** 4"–4' **Spread:** 6"–4' **Hardiness:** zones 3–10

Joe-Pye Weed
Eupatorium

These architectural plants add volume and stature to the garden and put on a good show of late-season flowers.

Growing

Joe-Pye weeds prefer **full sun to partial shade.** The soil should be **fertile** and **moist,** but wet soils are tolerated.

Tips

These plants can be used in a moist border or near a pond or other water feature. The tall types work well at the back of a border or in the center of a bed where they can create a backdrop for lower-growing plants.

Recommended

E. coelestinum (hardy ageratum) is a bushy, upright plant that bears clusters of light blue to lavender flowers.

E. maculatum (*E. purpureum*) is a large plant with reddish purple stems. It bears clusters of purple flowers. **'Gateway'** is a smaller plant with large clusters of deep pink flowers.

E. rugosum (*Ageratina altissima;* boneset, white snakeroot) forms a bushy, mounding clump of foliage and bears clusters of white flowers. **'Chocolate'** has dark purple leaves that mature to dark green.

Also called: boneset, snakeroot
Features: late-summer and fall flowers in white, purple, blue, pink or lavender; green to dark purple foliage; mounding to upright habit
Height: 2–10' **Spread:** 18"–4'
Hardiness: zones 3–9

E. rugosum (above), *E. maculatum* (below)

Joe-Pye weeds attract bees, butterflies and other pollinators to the garden in late summer.

Lady's Mantle
Alchemilla

A. *alpina* (above), A. *mollis* (below)

Few perennials are as captivating as a lady's mantle with droplets of morning dew clinging to its velvety leaves like shimmering pearls.

Growing

Lady's mantles grow well in **light or partial shade** with protection from the afternoon sun. The soil should be **fertile, humus rich, moist** and **well drained**. These plants dislike hot locations, and excessive sun can scorch the leaves. Leaves that look tired and heat stressed can be sheared back in summer; new leaves will emerge. Spent flowers can be removed to reduce self-seeding and to encourage additional blooming.

Tips

Ideal for grouping under trees in a woodland garden or along border and pathway edges, lady's mantles soften the bright colors of other plants. They also look attractive in containers. Compact selections are well suited to rock gardens.

Recommended

A. alpina (alpine lady's mantle) is a low-growing plant. Clusters of tiny, yellow flowers are borne in summer.

A. mollis (common lady's mantle) forms a mound of soft, rounded foliage and produces sprays of frothy-looking, yellowish green flowers in early summer.

The chartreuse yellow flower sprays of lady's mantle make interesting substitutes for baby's breath in fresh and dried arrangements.

Features: summer and early-fall flowers in yellow or yellow-green; attractive foliage; mounding or spreading habit **Height:** 3–18" **Spread:** 20–24" **Hardiness:** zones 3–7

Lavender

Lavandula

*L*avender is considered the queen of herbs. With both aromatic and ornamental qualities, it makes a valuable addition to any garden.

Growing

Lavenders grow best in **full sun**. The soil should be **average to fertile** and **alkaline**, and it must be **well drained**. Once established, lavenders tolerate heat and drought. A sheltered site or fall mulching protects lavenders from winter cold and wind. In early May, after the new growth has started, any dead branches should be removed. After flowering, the plants can be shaped more vigorously.

Tips

Lavenders are wonderful, aromatic edging plants. They can be planted in drifts, featured as specimens in small spaces or used to form low hedges.

Recommended

L. angustifolia (English lavender) is a bushy, aromatic plant. It bears spikes of light purple flowers from mid-summer to fall. The many cultivars include plants with white or pink flowers, silvery gray to olive green foliage and dwarf or compact habits.

L. x *intermedia* (lavandin) is a natural hybrid between the smaller English lavender and spike lavender (*L. latifolia*). The flowers are held on long spikes. Cultivars are available.

L. angustifolia (above & below)

Relaxing and soothing, the sensuous scent of lavender is used in aromatherapy, sachets and potpourris.

Features: fragrant, mid-summer and fall flowers in purple, pink, blue or white; fragrant evergreen foliage; bushy habit **Height:** 8–36" **Spread:** up to 4' **Hardiness:** zones 5–9

Meadow Rue
Thalictrum

Meadow rues are tall without being overbearing. Their fluffy flowers sway gracefully in the wind on wiry stems above fine foliage.

Growing

Meadow rues prefer **light or partial shade** but tolerate full sun if grown in moist soil. The soil should be **humus rich, moist** and **well drained**. Meadow rues dislike being disturbed, and they may take a while to re-establish if you do so.

Tips

Meadow rues look beautiful when naturalized in an open woodland or meadow garden. Placed in the middle or at the back of a border, they make a soft backdrop for bolder plants and flowers.

Mark where you plant meadow rues to avoid inadvertently disturbing their roots while cultivating before the plants emerge, which might not be until late spring.

T. aquilegifolium (above & below)

Tall meadow rues in exposed locations may need some support to prevent toppling by strong winds.

Recommended

T. aquilegifolium (columbine meadow rue) forms an upright mound with pink or white plumes of flowers. Cultivars are available.

T. rochebruneanum **'Lavender Mist'** (lavender mist meadow rue) forms a narrow, upright clump. The lavender purple blooms have numerous distinctive yellow stamens.

Features: summer flowers in pink, purple, yellow or white; light, airy habit; attractive foliage **Height:** 2–5' **Spread:** 12–36" **Hardiness:** zones 3–8

Meadowsweet

Filipendula

*or an impressive, informal, vertical accent and showy clusters of fluffy, fragrant flowers, meadowsweets are second to none.

Growing

Meadowsweets prefer **partial or light shade** but tolerate full sun in evenly moist soil. The soil should be **fertile, deep, humus rich** and **moist,** except for *F. vulgaris,* which tolerates dry soil. Divide in spring or fall.

Tips

Most meadowsweets are excellent for bog gardens or wet sites. Grow them alongside streams or in moist meadows. If they are well watered, meadowsweets may also be grown at the back of a border to create a billowy accent. Grow *F. vulgaris* if you can't provide the moisture the other species need.

Recommended

F. rubra (queen-of-the-prairie) forms a large, spreading clump and bears clusters of fragrant, pink flowers. Cultivars are available.

F. ulmaria (queen-of-the-meadow) forms a mounding clump with large clusters of cream white flowers. Cultivars include '**Aurea,**' with golden foliage, and '**Variegata,**' with variegated foliage of creamy yellow and dark green.

F. vulgaris (dropwort, meadowsweet) is a low-growing species that bears clusters of fragrant, cream white flowers. Cultivars such as '**Plena,**' with double flowers, and '**Rosea,**' with pink flowers, are available.

F. rubra (above), *F. ulmaria* (below)

Deadhead meadowsweets if you so desire, but the faded seedheads are quite attractive when left in place or used in dried flower arrangements.

Features: late-spring and summer flowers in white, cream, pink or red; attractive foliage
Height: 24"–8' **Spread:** 18"–4'
Hardiness: zones 3–8

Peony

Paeonia

P. *lactiflora* 'Shimmering Velvet' (above)
P. *l.* cultivars (below)

Place wire supports or peony cages around the plants in early spring to support the heavy flowers. The foliage will grow to hide the wire.

With their simple single flowers or extravagant doubles, it's easy to become mesmerized by the voluptuous peonies. Once the fleeting but magnificent flower display is done, the foliage remains stellar throughout the growing season.

Growing

Peonies prefer **full sun** but tolerate some shade. The planting site should be well prepared before the plants are introduced. Peonies like **fertile, humus-rich, moist, well-drained** soil with a lot of compost. Mulch peonies lightly with compost in spring and early fall. Too much fertilizer, particularly nitrogen, causes floppy growth and retards blooming. Deadhead to keep the plants looking tidy.

Tips

Peonies look great in a border combined with other early bloomers. The emerging peony foliage will hide the dying foliage of underplanted bulbs and other plants. Avoid planting peonies under trees, which compete for moisture and nutrients.

Tubers planted too shallowly or, more commonly, too deeply will not flower. The buds or eyes on the tuber should be 1½–2" below the soil surface.

Recommended

Peony selections number in the hundreds, with single or double, possibly fragrant flowers in a wide range of colors. Visit your local garden center to check availability.

Features: spring and early-summer flowers in white, cream, yellow, pink, red or purple; attractive foliage **Height:** 24–32" **Spread:** 24–32" **Hardiness:** zones 2–8

Pinks
Dianthus

D. deltoides (above), *D. plumarius* (below)

From tiny and delicate to large and robust, this genus contains a wide variety of plants, many with spice-scented flowers.

Growing

Pinks prefer **full sun** but tolerate some light shade. A **neutral or alkaline, well-drained** soil is required. The most important factor is drainage—pinks hate to stand in water. Rocky out-croppings make up the native habitat of many species.

Tips

Pinks are excellent for rock gardens and rock walls, and for edging borders and walkways. They can also be used in cutting gardens and even as groundcovers. To prolong blooming, deadhead as the flowers fade, but leave a few flowers to go to seed.

Recommended

D. x allwoodii (Allwood pinks) hybrids form compact mounds and bear flowers in a wide range of colors. Many cultivars are available.

D. deltoides (maiden pink) forms a mat of foliage with flowers in shades of red.

D. gratianopolitanus (cheddar pink) is long-lived and forms a very dense mat of evergreen, silver gray foliage with sweet-scented flowers mostly in shades of pink. It offers good winter interest.

D. plumarius (cottage pink) is note-worthy for its role in the development of many popular cultivars known collectively as garden pinks. The flowers can be single, semi-double or fully double and are available in many colors.

Features: possibly fragrant spring and summer flowers in pink, red, white or purple; attractive foliage **Height:** 2–18" **Spread:** 6–24" **Hardiness:** zones 3–9

Purple Coneflower
Echinacea

E. purpurea (above & below)

Purple coneflower attracts wildlife to the garden, providing pollen, nectar and seeds to various hungry visitors.

Purple coneflower is a visual delight, with its mauve petals offset by a spiky, orange center.

Growing
Purple coneflower grows well in **full sun** or very **light shade**. It tolerates any **well-drained** soil but prefers an **average to rich soil**. Its thick taproot makes this plant drought resistant, but it prefers to have regular water. Divide every four years or so in spring or fall.

Deadhead early in the season to prolong flowering. Later you may wish to leave the flowerheads in place to self-seed. Pinch plants back or thin out the stems in early summer to encourage bushy growth that is less prone to mildew.

Tips
Plant purple coneflower in meadow gardens and informal borders, either in groups or as single specimens.

The dry flowerheads make an interesting feature in fall and winter gardens and provide food for birds.

Recommended
E. purpurea is an upright plant covered in prickly hairs. It bears pinkish purple flowers with conical, orangy centers. Cultivars are available, including ones with white or pink flowers.

Features: mid-summer and fall flowers in purple, pink or white, with rusty orange centers; persistent seedheads **Height:** 2–5' **Spread:** 12–24" **Hardiness:** zones 3–8

Russian Sage
Perovskia

Russian sage offers four-season interest: soft, gray-green leaves on light gray stems in spring; fuzzy, violet blue flowers in summer; and silvery white stems in fall that last until late winter.

Growing

Russian sage prefers **full sun**. The soil should be **poor to moderately fertile** and **well drained**. Too much water and nitrogen will cause this plant's growth to flop, so do not plant it next to heavy feeders. Because it is a subshrub that originates from a single stem, Russian sage cannot be divided.

In spring, when new growth appears low on the branches, or in fall, cut the plant back hard to about 6–12" to encourage vigorous, bushy growth.

P. atriplicifolia (above), *P. a.* 'Filgran' (below)

Tips

The silvery foliage and blue flowers work well with other plants in the back of a mixed border and soften the appearance of daylilies. Russian sage can also create a soft screen in a natural garden or on a dry bank.

Recommended

P. atriplicifolia is a loose, upright plant with silvery white, finely divided foliage. The small, lavender blue flowers are loosely held on silvery, branched stems. Cultivars are available.

Russian sage blossoms make a lovely addition to fresh bouquets and dried-flower arrangements.

Features: mid-summer and fall flowers in blue or purple; attractive habit; fragrant, gray-green foliage **Height:** 36"–4' **Spread:** 36"–4' **Hardiness:** zones 4–9

Sedum

Sedum

S. *spectibile* 'Brilliant' (above), S. 'Autumn Joy' (below)

Some 300 to 500 species of sedum are distributed throughout the Northern Hemisphere. Many sedums are grown for their foliage, which can range in color from steel gray-blue and green to red and burgundy.

Growing

Sedums prefer **full sun** but tolerate partial shade. The soil should be of **average fertility,** very **well drained** and **neutral to alkaline**. Divide in spring when needed.

Tips

Low-growing sedums make wonderful groundcovers and additions to rock

Early-summer pruning of upright species and hybrids encourages compact, bushy growth, but it can also delay flowering.

gardens or rock walls. They also edge beds and borders beautifully. Taller sedums give a lovely late-season display in a bed or border.

Recommended

S. acre (gold moss stonecrop) is a low-growing, wide-spreading plant that bears small, yellow-green flowers.

S. **'Autumn Joy'** (autumn joy sedum) is a popular upright hybrid. The flowers open pink or red and later fade to deep bronze.

S. spectabile (showy stonecrop) is an upright species with pink flowers. Cultivars are available.

S. spurium (two-row stonecrop) forms a low, wide mat of foliage with deep pink or white flowers. The many cultivars available are often grown for their colorful foliage.

Also called: stonecrop
Features: summer and fall flowers in yellow, white, red or pink; decorative, fleshy foliage
Height: 2–24" **Spread:** 12–24" or more
Hardiness: zones 3–8

Silphium

Silphium

S. perfoliatum (above & below)

Silphiums are no shrinking violets! Given the right cultural conditions, these native prairie or meadow plants can reach heights of 8–10'.

Growing

Silphiums grow well in **full sun** or **partial shade** but will flop in excessive shade. The soil should be of **average fertility, neutral to alkaline** and **moist**. They tolerate heavy clay soils. The plants can be divided in spring, but the large root mass may require the efforts of two people to divide it.

Tips

These tall plants can be used in prairie and meadow plantings, at the back of borders, along the edges of woodland gardens, in bog gardens and in waterside plantings.

Recommended

S. laciniatum (compass plant) forms an upright clump of hairy stems. It bears clusters of yellow, daisy-like flowers in late summer and fall.

S. perfoliatum (cup plant) forms an upright clump of hairless stems. From mid-summer to fall, it bears clusters of yellow, daisy-like flowers with darker centers.

Also called: compass plant
Features: yellow flowers in summer and fall; adaptable to varied growing conditions; large size **Height:** 8–10' **Spread:** 3–5'
Hardiness: zones 5–9

Yarrow

Achillea

A. millefolium 'Paprika' (above)
A. filipendulina hybrid (above)

Yarrows make excellent groundcovers and are popular, water-efficient additions to xeriscapes. When dried, the flowers retain a touch of their original colors.

Yarrows are informal, tough plants with flowers in a fantastic range of colors.

Growing

Yarrows grow best in **full sun**. The soil should be of **average fertility, sandy** and **well drained**. These plants tolerate drought and poor soil. They also tolerate heavy, wet soil and high humidity, but they do not thrive in these conditions. Excessively rich soil or too much nitrogen results in weak, floppy growth and a shorter life span.

Deadhead to prolong blooming or shear the plant back after the first flush of blooms. Basal foliage should be left in place over winter and tidied up in spring.

Tips

Cottage gardens, wildflower gardens and mixed borders are perfect places for these informal plants. They thrive in hot, dry locations where not much else grows.

Recommended

A. filipendulina (fernleaf yarrow) forms a clump of ferny foliage and bears yellow flowers. It has been used to develop many hybrids and cultivars.

A. millefolium **hybrids** (common yarrow) forms a clump or mat of soft, finely divided foliage and bears white flowers. The many popular cultivars offer flowers in a wide range of interesting colors, and some are multicolored.

Features: mid-summer and fall flowers in white, yellow, red, orange, pink, purple or multicolored; attractive foliage; spreading or clumping habit. **Height:** 4"–4'
Spread: 12–36" **Hardiness:** zones 3–9

Aronia

Aronia

A. m. 'Autumn Magic' (above), A. melanocarpa (below)

These lovely shrubs deserve to be more widely planted. With clusters of white flowers in spring, glossy foliage that turns orange and red in fall and decorative fruit that persists all winter, aronias have something to offer year-round.

Growing

Aronias grow well in **full sun** or **partial shade,** with best flowering and fruiting in full sun. The soil should be of **average fertility** and **well drained,** although the plants adapt to most soil conditions. Wet, dry or poor soil conditions are tolerated.

Tips

Aronias are useful shrubs to include in shrub and mixed borders, and they make interesting, low-maintenance specimen plants. Left to their own devices, they can colonize a fairly large area.

Recommended

A. ***arbutifolia*** (red chokeberry) is an upright shrub that bears white flowers in late spring and bright red, waxy fruit in fall. The glossy, dark green foliage turns red in fall. Cultivars are available.

A. ***melanocarpa*** (black chokeberry) is an upright, suckering shrub native to the eastern U.S. The white flowers of late spring are followed by black fruit in fall. The glossy, green foliage turns bright red to purple in fall. Cultivars are available.

Also called: chokeberry **Features:** attractive white spring flowers; fall fruit; colorful fall foliage **Habit:** suckering, deciduous shrub **Height:** 3–6' **Spread:** 3–10' **Hardiness:** zones 3–8

Barberry

Berberis

B. thunbergii 'Aurea' (above), *B. thunbergii* (below)

The variations available in plant size, foliage color and fruit make barberry a real workhorse of the plant world.

Growing

Barberry develops the best fall color when grown in **full sun**, but it tolerates partial shade. Any **well-drained** soil is suitable. This plant tolerates drought and urban conditions but suffers in poorly drained, wet soil.

Tips

Large barberry plants make great barrier or security hedges with formidable prickles. Barberry can also be included in shrub and mixed borders. Small cultivars can be grown in rock gardens, in raised beds and along rock walls.

Recommended

B. thunbergii (Japanese barberry) is a dense shrub with a broad, rounded habit. The bright green foliage turns variable shades of orange, red or purple in fall. Yellow spring flowers are followed by glossy, red fruit later in summer. Many cultivars have been developed for their variable foliage color, including shades of purple or yellow and variegated.

Japanese barberry (along with its cultivars) has been placed on Ohio's list of invasive plants. If you live next to a woodland or forest, consider not planting shrubs that are on this list.

Features: attractive foliage; yellow flowers; fruit **Habit:** prickly, deciduous shrub
Height: 1–6' **Spread:** 18"–6'
Hardiness: zones 4–8

Beech

Fagus

F. sylvatica 'Pendula' (above), *F. sylvatica* (below)

The aristocrats of the large shade trees, the majestic beeches are attractive at any age, from their big, bold, beautiful youth through to their slow, craggy decline.

Growing

Beeches grow equally well in **full sun** or **partial shade**. The soil should be of **average fertility, loamy** and **well drained,** although almost any well-drained soil is tolerated.

American beech doesn't like having its roots disturbed and should be transplanted only when very young. European beech transplants easily and tolerates more varied soil conditions than American beech.

Tips

Beeches make excellent specimens. They are also used as shade trees and in woodland gardens. These trees need a lot of space, but the European beech's adaptability to pruning makes it a reasonable choice in a small garden.

Recommended

F. grandifolia (American beech) is a broad-canopied tree native to most of eastern North America.

F. sylvatica (European beech) is a spectacular broad tree. Among the interesting cultivars are trees small enough to be used in the home garden, and narrow columnar and weeping selections are available. The foliage can be purple, yellow or variegated in pink, white and green.

Beechnuts are edible raw or roasted.

Features: attractive foliage; smooth bark; varied habit; fall color; fruit **Habit:** large, oval, deciduous shade tree **Height:** 30–80'
Spread: 10–65' **Hardiness:** zones 4–8

Buckeye
Aesculus

A. *parviflora* (above), A. *hippocastanum* (below)

Buckeyes range from trees with immense regal bearing to small but impressive shrubs. All have spectacular flowers.

The heavy shade of buckeyes and horsechestnuts is excellent for cooling buildings but makes it difficult to grow grass underneath.

Growing

Buckeyes grow well in **full sun** or **partial shade**. The soil should be **fertile, moist** and **well drained**. These trees dislike excessive drought.

Tips

Buckeyes are used as specimen and shade trees. The roots of buckeyes can break up sidewalks and patios if planted too close.

The smaller, shrubby buckeyes grow well near pond plantings and also make interesting specimens. Give them plenty of space, because they can form large colonies.

Do not eat the nuts of any of the *Aesculus* species. They are poisonous.

Recommended

A. glabra (Ohio buckeye), our state tree, is lovely in flower, but disease often causes early leaf drop. (Zones 3–7)

A. hippocastanum (common horse-chestnut) is a large, rounded tree that will branch right to the ground if grown in an open setting. The flowers, white with yellow or pink marks, are borne in long spikes. (Zones 3–7)

A. parviflora (bottlebrush buckeye) is a spreading, mound-forming, suckering shrub that produces plentiful spikes of creamy white flowers. (Zones 4–9)

A. pavia (red buckeye) is a low-growing to rounded, shrubby tree with cherry red flowers and handsome foliage. It needs consistent moisture. (Zones 4–8)

Also called: horsechestnut
Features: attractive early-summer flowers in yellow, white or cream; bold foliage; spiny fruit
Habit: rounded or spreading, deciduous tree or shrub **Height:** 8–80' **Spread:** 8–65'
Hardiness: zones 3–9

Butterfly Bush
Buddleia (Buddleja)

The fragrant flowers of these attractive bushes will attract countless butterflies to your garden, along with a wide variety of other pollinating insects.

Growing
Butterfly bushes prefer to grow in **full sun,** producing few if any flowers in shady conditions. The soil should be **fertile to average** and **well drained**. These plants tolerate drought once established. Because they flower on the current year's growth, even plants killed back over winter will bloom.

Tips
Butterfly bushes make beautiful additions to shrub and mixed borders. The graceful arching habit makes them ideal as specimen plants. The dwarf forms that stay under 5' are suitable for small gardens.

Recommended
B. davidii (orange-eye butterfly bush, summer lilac) is the most commonly grown species. It grows 4–10' tall, with an equal spread. It bears fragrant flowers in bright and pastel shades of purple, pink, blue and white from mid-summer through fall. Many cultivars are available.

B. x *weyeriana* is a wide-spreading shrub with arching stems. It grows 6–12' tall, spreads 5–10' and bears purple or yellow flowers from mid-summer through fall. Cultivars are available. (Zones 6–9)

B. davidii (above & below)

Butterfly bushes are among the best shrubs for attracting butterflies and bees to your garden. Avoid spraying them for pests so as not to harm these beautiful and beneficial insects.

Features: attractive purple, pink, blue, white or yellow flowers; arching habit
Habit: large, deciduous shrub with arching branches **Height:** 4–12' **Spread:** 4–10'
Hardiness: zones 5–9

Cherry • Plum • Almond
Prunus

P. subhirtella 'Pendula Rosea' (above)

Cherries are so beautiful and uplifting after the gray days of winter that few gardeners can resist them.

Growing
These flowering fruit trees prefer **full sun**. The soil should be of **average fertility, moist** and **well drained**. Shallow roots will emerge from the lawn if the tree is not getting sufficient water.

Tips
Prunus species are beautiful as specimen plants, and many are small enough to be included in almost any garden. Small species and cultivars can also be included in borders or grouped to form informal hedges or barriers. Pissard plum and purpleleaf sand cherry can be trained as formal hedges.

Because pest problems afflict many of the cherries, they can be rather short-lived. Choose resistant species such as Sargent cherry or Higan cherry. If you plant a more susceptible species, such as the Japanese flowering cherry, enjoy it while it thrives but be prepared to replace it.

Recommended
A few popular selections from among the many species, hybrids and cultivars available are given here. Check with your local nursery or garden center for other possible selections.

P. cerasifera '**Atropurpurea**' (Pissard plum) and *P.* x *cistena* (purpleleaf sand cherry) are shrubby plants grown for their purple foliage and light pink flowers.

P. sargentii (Sargent cherry), *P. serrulata* (Japanese flowering cherry) and *P. subhirtella* (Higan cherry) are rounded or spreading trees grown for their white or light pink flowers as well as often-attractive bark and bright red or yellow fall color.

Features: attractive spring to early-summer flowers in pink or white; fruit; often-attractive bark; fall foliage. **Habit:** upright, rounded, spreading or weeping, deciduous tree or shrub **Height:** 4–75' **Spread:** 4–50' **Hardiness:** zones 2–8

Cotoneaster

Cotoneaster

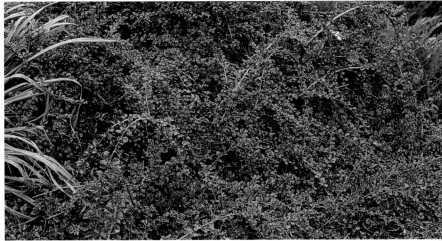

C. apiculatus (above), *C. dammeri* (below)

With their diverse sizes, shapes, flowers, fruit and foliage, cotoneasters are so versatile that if they weren't so lovely they would border on being overused.

Growing

Cotoneasters grow well in **full sun** or **partial shade**. The soil should be of **average fertility** and **well drained**.

Tips

Cotoneasters can be included in shrub or mixed borders. Low spreaders work well as groundcovers, and shrubby species can be used to form hedges. Larger species are grown as small specimen trees, and some low growers are grafted onto standards and grown as small, weeping trees.

Recommended

Many cotoneasters are available. Just a few possibilities are described below. Your local garden center will be able to help you find one suitable for your garden.

C. adpressus (creeping cotoneaster), *C.* x **'Hessei'** and *C. horizontalis* (rockspray cotoneaster) are low-growing groundcover plants.

C. apiculatus (cranberry cotoneaster) and *C. dammeri* (bearberry cotoneaster) are widespreading, low, shrubby plants.

C. salicifolius (willowleaf cotoneaster) is an upright, shrubby plant that can be trained to form a small tree.

Features: attractive foliage; early-summer flowers in white or pink; persistent fruit; variety of forms **Habit:** evergreen or deciduous groundcover, shrub or small tree **Height:** 6"–15' **Spread:** 3–12' **Hardiness:** zones 4–8

Crabapple
Malus

Abundant spring flowers, exceptional tolerance for winter cold and summer heat, plus colorful fruit that often persists through winter—what more could anyone ask from a small tree?

Growing
Crabapples prefer **full sun** but tolerate partial shade. The soil should be of **average to rich fertility, moist** and **well drained**. These trees tolerate damp soil but suffer in wet locations.

One of the best ways to prevent the spread of crabapple pests and diseases is to clean up the fallen leaves and fruit. Many pests overwinter in the fruit, leaves or soil at the base of the tree. Clearing away their winter shelter helps keep their populations under control.

Tips
Crabapples make excellent specimen plants. Many varieties are quite small, so there is one to suit almost any size of garden. Some forms are even small enough to grow in large containers. The flexibility of the young branches makes these trees good choices for creating espalier specimens.

Recommended
Crabapple species, varieties and cultivars number in the hundreds. One of the most important attributes to look for is disease resistance. Even the most beautiful flowers, fruit or habit will never look good if the plant is ravaged by pests or diseases. Ask for information about new, resistant cultivars at your local nursery or garden center.

Features: attractive white to deep pink spring flowers; persistent, yellow to red late-season and winter fruit; fall foliage; attractive habit; scaly bark **Habit:** rounded, mounded or spreading, small to medium, deciduous tree **Height:** 5–30' **Spread:** 6–30' **Hardiness:** zones 4–8

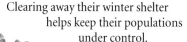

Dogwood
Cornus

Stem color, leaf variegation, fall color, growth habit, soil adaptability and hardiness are all positive attributes to be found in the dogwoods.

Growing

Dogwoods grow well in **full sun, light shade** or **partial shade,** with a slight preference for light shade. The soil should be of **average to high fertility, high in organic matter, neutral to slightly acidic** and **well drained**.

Tips

Shrub dogwoods can be included in a shrub or mixed border. They look best in groups rather than as single specimens. The tree species make wonderful specimen plants and are small enough to include in most gardens. Use them along the edge of a woodland, in a shrub or mixed border, alongside a house, or near a water feature or patio.

Recommended

C. alba (red-twig dogwood, Tartarian dogwood) and *C. sericea* (*C. stolonifera*; red-osier dogwood) species and cultivars are grown for their bright red, orange or yellow stems. The fall foliage color can be attractive. (Zones 2–8)

C. alternifolia (pagoda dogwood) can be grown as a large, multi-stemmed shrub or a small, single-stemmed tree. The branches have an attractive layered appearance. Clusters of small, white flowers appear in early summer. (Zones 3–8)

Features: late-spring to early-summer flowers in white or pink; fall foliage; colorful stems; fruit **Habit:** deciduous, large shrub or small tree **Height:** 5–30' **Spread:** 5–30' **Hardiness:** zones 2–9

C. alba 'Bailhalo' (above)
C. kousa var. *chinensis* (below)

C. florida (flowering dogwood) graces our woods with its beautiful horizontally layered habit and showy flowers. Ask your county cooperative extension office if anthracnose infections have been a problem in your area, because these trees are susceptible. (Zones 5–9)

C. kousa (Kousa dogwood) is grown for its white-bracted flowers, edible bright red fruit, red or purple fall color and interesting bark. **Var.** *chinensis* (Chinese dogwood) grows more vigorously and has larger flowers. (Zones 5–9)

Elder
Sambucus

S. canadensis (above), S. racemosa (below)

Both the flowers and the fruit can be used to make wine. The berries are popular for pies and jelly. The raw berries are marginally edible but not palatable and can cause stomach upset, particularly in children. All other parts of elders are toxic.

Elders work well in a naturalized garden. Cultivars are available that will provide light texture in a dark area, dark foliage in a bright area or variegated yellow foliage and bright stems in brilliant sunshine.

Growing
Elders grow well in **full sun** or **partial shade,** but plants grown for colorful foliage develop the best color in **light or partial shade**. The soil should be of **average fertility, moist** and **well drained,** but established elders tolerate dry soil.

Tips
Elders can be used in a shrub or mixed border, in a natural woodland garden or next to a pond or other water feature. Types with interesting or colorful foliage can be used as specimen plants or focal points.

Recommended
S. canadensis (American elder/elderberry), *S. nigra* (European elder/elderberry, black elder/elderberry) and *S. racemosa* (European red elder/elderberry) are rounded shrubs with white or pinkish white flowers followed by red or dark purple berries. Cultivars are available with green, yellow, bronze or purple foliage and deeply divided to feathery foliage.

Also called: elderberry **Features:** attractive white to pinkish early-summer flowers; fruit; divided to feathery foliage **Habit:** large, bushy, deciduous shrub **Height:** 5–20' **Spread:** 5–20' **Hardiness:** zones 3–9

False Cypress
Chamaecyparis

Conifer shoppers are blessed with a marvelous selection of false cypresses that offer color, size, shape and growth habits not available in most other evergreens.

Growing

False cypresses prefer **full sun,** but will tolerate light shade, especially the gold and variegated cultivars . The soil should be **fertile, moist, neutral to acidic** and **well drained**, although alkaline soils are tolerated. In shaded areas, growth may be sparse or thin.

Tips

Tree varieties are used as specimen plants and for hedging. The dwarf and slow-growing cultivars are used in borders, in rock gardens and as bonsai. False cypress shrubs can be grown near the house or as evergreen specimens in large containers.

Recommended

False cypresses come in several species and many cultivars. The scaly foliage can be in a drooping or strand-like form, in fan-like or feathery sprays and may be dark green, bright green or yellow. Plant forms vary too, from mounding or rounded to tall and pyramidal, or narrow with pendulous branches. Check with your local garden center or nursery to see what is available.

C. pisifera 'Mops' (above), *C. nootkatensis* 'Pendula' (below)

The oils in the foliage of false cypresses may irritate sensitive skin.

Features: attractive foliage; varied habits; cones **Habit:** narrow, pyramidal to small, rounded, evergreen tree or shrub **Height:** 18"–150' **Spread:** 18"–80' **Hardiness:** zones 4–8

Fothergilla
Fothergilla

F. major (above & below)

Flowers, fragrance, fall color and interesting soft tan to brownish stems give fothergillas year-round appeal.

Growing

Fothergillas grow well in **full sun** or **partial shade,** but full sun produces the most flowers and the best fall color. The soil should be of **average fertility, acidic, humus rich, moist** and **well drained**.

Tips

Fothergillas are attractive and useful in shrub or mixed borders, in woodland gardens and when combined with evergreen groundcover.

Recommended

F. gardenii (dwarf fothergilla) is a bushy shrub that bears fragrant, white flowers. The foliage turns yellow, orange and red in fall. Cultivars are available.

F. major (large fothergilla) is a larger, rounded shrub that bears fragrant, white flowers. The autumn colors are yellow, orange and scarlet. Cultivars are available.

Fothergilla bears bottlebrush-shaped flowers with a delicate honey scent. These generally problem-free shrubs make wonderful companions to azaleas, rhododendrons and other acid-loving woodland plants.

Features: attractive, fragrant, white flowers in spring; fall foliage **Habit:** dense, rounded or bushy, deciduous shrub **Height:** 2–10' **Spread:** 2–10' **Hardiness:** zones 4–9

Fringe Tree
Chionanthus

C. virginicus (above & below)

Cold hardy and adaptable to a wide range of growing conditions, fringe trees become densely covered in silky white, honey-scented flowers that shimmer in the wind over a long period in spring.

Growing

Fringe trees prefer **full sun**. They do best in soil that is **fertile, acidic, moist** and **well drained** but adapt to most soil conditions. In the wild they are often found growing alongside stream banks.

Tips

Fringe trees work well as specimen plants, as part of a border or beside a water -feature. They begin flowering at a very young age.

Recommended

C. retusus (Chinese fringe tree) is a rounded, spreading shrub or small tree with deeply furrowed, peeling bark and erect clusters of fragrant, white flowers. (Zones 5–9)

C. virginicus (white fringe tree) is a spreading small tree or large shrub with smooth bark that bears drooping, fragrant, white flowers.

Fringe trees can be very difficult to find in general nurseries. Specialty nurseries and plant sales at botanical gardens, universities or colleges are the most likely places to find them.

Features: attractive white flowers in early summer; furrowed or smooth bark
Habit: rounded or spreading, deciduous, large shrub or small tree **Height:** 10–25'
Spread: 10–25' **Hardiness:** zones 4–9

Ginkgo
Ginkgo

G. biloba (above & below)

Be patient with ginkgo. Its gawky, irregularly angular youth will eventually pass to reveal a spectacular mature specimen.

Growing
Ginkgo prefers **full sun**. The soil should be **fertile, sandy** and **well drained,** but this tree adapts to most conditions. It is also tolerant of urban conditions and cold weather.

Tips
Although its growth is very slow, Ginkgo eventually becomes a large tree that is best suited for use as a specimen tree in parks and large gardens. It can be used as a street tree.

If you buy an unnamed plant, be sure it has been propagated from cuttings. Seed-grown trees may prove to be female, and the stinky fruit is not something you want dropping all over your lawn, driveway or sidewalk.

Recommended
G. biloba is variable in habit. The uniquely fan-shaped leaves can turn an attractive shade of yellow in fall. Several cultivars are available.

Because the fruits have a very unpleasant odor, female ginkgos are generally avoided.

Also called: ginko, maidenhair tree
Features: attractive summer and fall foliage; furrowed bark **Habit:** deciduous tree, conical in youth and variable with age
Height: 40–100' **Spread:** 10–100'
Hardiness: zones 3–9

Golden Rain Tree

Koereutaria

K. paniculata (above & below)

With its delicate clusters of yellow flowers and overall lacy appearance in summer, this lovely tree deserves wider use as a specimen or shade tree.

Growing

Golden rain tree grows best in **full sun**. The soil should be **average to fertile, moist** and **well drained**. This fast-growing tree tolerates heat, drought, wind and polluted air. It also adapts to most alkaline or acidic soils.

Tips

Golden rain tree makes an excellent shade or specimen tree for small properties. Its ability to adapt to a wide range of soils makes it useful in many garden situations. The fruit is not messy and will not stain patios or decks.

Recommended

K. paniculata is an attractive, rounded, spreading tree. It bears long clusters of small, yellow flowers in mid-summer, followed by green capsular fruit with red tinges. The attractive leaves are somewhat lacy in appearance and may turn bright yellow in fall. Cultivars are available.

This Asian species is one of the few trees with yellow flowers and one of the only trees to bloom in mid- or late summer.

Features: attractive habit, foliage, flowers and fruit **Habit:** rounded, spreading, deciduous tree **Height:** 30–40' **Spread:** 30–40' **Hardiness:** zones 5–8

Hawthorn

Crataegus

C. phaenopyrum (above)
C. laevigata 'Paul's Scarlet' (below)

The hawthorns are uncommonly beautiful trees that offer a generous spring show of lovely apple-like blossoms that yield persistent, glossy, red fruit and often have good fall color.

Growing

Hawthorns grow equally well in **full sun** or **partial shade**. They adapt to any **well-drained** soil and tolerate urban conditions.

Tips

Hawthorns can be grown as specimen plants or hedges in urban sites, lakeside gardens and exposed locations. They are popular in areas where vandalism is a problem, because very few people wish to grapple with plants bearing stiff, 2" long thorns. If children play nearby, consider the mostly thornless *C. viridis* 'Winter King.'

If you dislike the pungent, overpowering scent of the May flowers, avoid planting hawthorn near a patio or bedroom window.

Recommended

C. laevigata (*C. oxycantha*; English hawthorn) is a low-branching, rounded tree with zigzag layers of thorny branches. It bears white or pink flowers that yield red fruit in late summer. Many cultivars are available.

C. phaenopyrum (*C. cordata*; Washington hawthorn) is an oval to rounded, thorny tree that bears white flowers and persistent, shiny, red fruit in fall. The glossy, green foliage turns red and orange in fall.

C. viridis **'Winter King'** (Winter King hawthorn) is a medium-sized tree with a wide, oval habit. It is prized for its show of white spring flowers, silvery bark and brilliant display of large, red fruit that persists through winter.

Features: late-spring or early-summer flowers; fruit; attractive foliage; thorny branches
Habit: rounded, deciduous tree, often with a zigzagged, layered branch pattern
Height: 15–35' **Spread:** 12–35'
Hardiness: zones 3–8

Holly

Ilex

Hollies vary greatly in shape and size and can be such delights when placed with full consideration for their needs.

Growing

These plants prefer **full sun** but tolerate partial shade. The soil should be of **average to rich fertility, humus rich** and **moist.** Hollies perform best in **acidic** soil with a pH of 6.5 or lower. Shelter hollies from winter wind to help prevent their evergreen leaves from drying out. Apply a summer mulch to keep the roots cool and moist.

Tips

Hollies can be used in groups, in woodland gardens and in shrub and mixed borders. They can also be shaped into hedges. Winterberry is good for naturalizing in moist sites.

I. x *meserveae* hybrid (above), *I.* x *meserveae* 'Blue Girl' (below)

Recommended

I. glabra (inkberry) is a rounded shrub with glossy, deep green, evergreen foliage and dark purple fruit. Cultivars are available. (Zones 4–9)

I. x *meserveae* (meserve holly, blue holly) is a group of hybrids that originated from crosses between tender English holly (*I. aquifolium*) and hardy hollies such as prostrate holly (*I. rugosa*). These dense, evergreen shrubs may be erect, mounding or spreading. (Zones 5–8)

I. verticillata (winterberry, winterberry holly) is a deciduous native species grown for its explosion of red fruit that persists into winter. Many cultivars and hybrids are available.

All hollies have male and female flowers on separate plants, and both must be present for the females to set fruit. One male plant will adequately pollinate two or three females.

Features: attractive glossy, sometimes spiny foliage; fruit; dense habit **Habit:** erect or spreading, evergreen or deciduous shrub or tree **Height:** 3–50' **Spread:** 3–40' **Hardiness:** zones 3–9

Hornbeam

Carpinus

C. caroliniana (above), C. betulus 'Fastgiata' (below)

Even through the oppressive humidity of summer, hornbeam leaves retain their bright, fresh green color.

The attractive and slow-growing hornbeams are related to the birches and filberts. They put on an interesting display of male catkins from late summer through winter.

Growing

Hornbeams prefer **full sun** but tolerate partial or light shade. The soil should be **average to fertile** and **well drained**.

Tips

These small- to medium-sized trees can be used as specimens or shade trees in small gardens. The narrow, upright cultivars are often used to create barriers and wind-breaks. *C. betulus* and its cultivars can be pruned to form large hedges.

Recommended

C. betulus (European hornbeam) is a pyramidal to rounded tree. The foliage turns bright yellow or orange in fall. Many cultivars are available, including narrow, upright and weeping selections. (Zones 5–7)

C. caroliniana (American horn-beam, ironwood, musclewood, bluebeech) is a small, slow-growing tree that tolerates shade and urban conditions. The foliage turns yellow to red or purple in fall. (Zones 3–9)

Features: attractive fall color **Habit:** pyramidal, deciduous tree **Height:** 10–65' **Spread:** 10–50' **Hardiness:** zones 3–8

Hydrangea
Hydrangea

Hydrangeas have many attractive qualities, including showy, often long-lasting flowers and glossy, green leaves, some of which turn beautiful colors in fall.

Growing

Hydrangeas grow well in **full sun** or **partial shade,** and some species tolerate full shade. The soil should be of **average to high fertility, humus rich, moist** and **well drained**. These plants perform best in cool, moist conditions. Shade or partial shade will reduce leaf and flower scorch in especially hot gardens.

Tips

Hydrangeas come in many forms and have a multitude of uses in the landscape. They can be included in shrub or mixed borders, used as informal barriers, planted as specimens or in groups or placed in containers.

Recommended

H. arborescens (smooth hydrangea) is a rounded shrub that flowers well even in shady conditions. Its much-preferred cultivars bear large clusters of showy white blossoms.

H. paniculata (panicle hydrangea) is a spreading to upright, large shrub or small tree that bears white flowers from late summer to early fall. **'Grandiflora'** (Peegee hydrangea) is one of the many available cultivars.

H. quercifolia (oakleaf hydrangea) is a mound-forming shrub with attractive, exfoliating, cinnamon brown bark. The

H. quercifolia (above), *H. paniculata* 'Grandiflora' (below)

large, lobed, oak-like leaves turn bronze to bright red in fall. This species has conical clusters of sterile and fertile flowers. The white sterile flowers mature to pink or pinkish purple.

Features: attractive flowers, foliage and bark **Habit:** deciduous, mounding or spreading shrub or tree **Height:** 3–80' **Spread:** 3–20' **Hardiness:** zones 4–9

Juniper
Juniperus

J. virginiana 'Blue Arrow' (above)
J. horizontalis 'Blue Prince' (below)

There may be a juniper in every gardener's future, with all the choices available, from low, creeping plants to upright, pyramidal forms.

Juniper 'berries' are poisonous if eaten in large quantities.

Growing

Junipers prefer **full sun** but tolerate light shade. Ideally, the soil should be of **average fertility** and **well drained,** but these plants tolerate most conditions.

Tips

The wide variety of junipers available have endless uses. They make prickly barriers and hedges, and they can be used in borders, as specimens or in groups. The large species can be used to form windbreaks, and the low-growing species can be used in rock gardens and as groundcovers.

Recommended

Junipers vary, not just from species to species, but often within a species. Cultivars are available for all species and may differ significantly from the species.

J. chinensis (Chinese juniper) is a conical tree or spreading shrub.

J. horizontalis (creeping juniper) is a prostrate, creeping groundcover.

J. procumbens (Japanese garden juniper) is a wide-spreading, stiff-branched, low shrub.

J. scopulorum (Rocky Mountain juniper) can be upright, rounded, weeping or spreading.

J. squamata (singleseed juniper) forms a prostrate or low, spreading shrub or a small, upright tree.

J. virginiana (eastern redcedar) is a durable, upright or wide-spreading tree.

Features: evergreen; variable habit; tolerates difficult growing conditions **Habit:** conical or columnar tree, rounded or spreading shrub or prostrate groundcover **Height:** 4"–80'
Spread: 18"–25' **Hardiness:** zones 3–9

Katsura-Tree
Cercidiphyllum

Katsura-tree adds distinction and grace to the garden. Even in youth it is poised and elegant, and it is bound to become a bewitching mature specimen.

Growing

Katsura-tree grows equally well in **full sun** or **partial shade**. The soil should be **fertile, humus rich, neutral to acidic, moist** and **well drained**. In order to become established, a newly planted tree must be watered regularly during dry spells for the first two years.

Tips

Katsura-tree is useful as a specimen or shade tree. The species is quite large and is best used in large gardens. The cultivar **'Pendula,'** although it spreads quite wide, can be used in smaller gardens.

Recommended

C. japonicum is a slow-growing tree with heart-shaped, blue-green leaves that turn yellow and orange in fall and develop a spicy scent. **'Pendula'** is one of the most elegant weeping trees available. It is usually grafted to a standard, and the mounding, cascading branches give the entire tree the appearance of a waterfall tumbling over rocks.

C. j. 'Pendula' (above), *C. japonicum* (below)

Katsura-tree is native to eastern Asia, and its delicate foliage blends well into Japanese-style gardens.

Features: attractive summer and fall foliage
Habit: rounded, spreading or weeping, often multi-stemmed, deciduous tree
Height: 10–65' **Spread:** 10–65'
Hardiness: zones 4–8

Lilac

Syringa

S. *meyeri* (above), S. *vulgaris* (below)

The hardest thing about growing lilacs is choosing from the many species and hundreds of cultivars available.

Requiring frost in order to flower, lilacs don't bloom in the warm southern parts of the U.S.

Growing

Lilacs grow best in **full sun**. The soil should be **fertile, humus rich** and **well drained**. These plants tolerate open, windy locations.

Tips

Include lilacs in a shrub or mixed border or use them to create an informal hedge. Japanese tree lilac can be used as a specimen tree.

Recommended

S. x *hyacinthiflora* (hyacinth-flowered lilac, early-flowering lilac) is a group of hardy, upright hybrids that become spreading as they mature. Clusters of fragrant flowers appear two weeks earlier than those of the French lilacs. The leaves turn reddish purple in fall. Many cultivars are available. (Zones 3–7)

S. meyeri (Meyer lilac) is a compact, rounded shrub that bears fragrant flowers in pink or lavender. (Zones 3–7)

S. reticulata (Japanese tree lilac) is a rounded, large shrub or small tree that bears white flowers. 'Ivory Silk' has a more compact habit and produces more flowers than the species. (Zones 3–7)

S. vulgaris (French lilac, common lilac) is the most familiar lilac. It is a suckering, spreading shrub with an irregular habit that bears fragrant, lilac-colored flowers. Hundreds of cultivars with a variety of flower colors are available. (Zones 2–8)

Features: attractive late-spring to mid-summer flowers in shades of purple, blue, pink and white **Habit:** variable deciduous shrub or small tree **Height:** 3–30' **Spread:** 3–25' **Hardiness:** zones 2–8

Linden

Tilia

Lindens are picturesque shade trees with a signature gum-drop shape and sweet-scented flowers that seem to capture the essence of summer.

Growing

Lindens grow best in **full sun**. The soil should be **average to fertile, moist** and **well drained**. These trees prefer an **alkaline** soil, but they adapt to most pH levels. They tolerate pollution and urban conditions.

Tips

Lindens are useful and attractive street trees, shade trees and specimen trees. Their tolerance of pollution and their moderate size make lindens ideal for city gardens.

Recommended

T. cordata (littleleaf linden) is a dense, pyramidal tree that may become rounded with age. It bears small, fragrant flowers with narrow, yellow-green bracts. Cultivars are available.

T. tomentosa (silver linden) has a broadly pyramidal or rounded habit. The small flowers are fragrant, and the glossy, green leaves have fuzzy, silvery undersides.

T. cordata (above)

Many people enjoy an herbal tea made with linden flowers.

Features: attractive foliage; fragrant flowers
Habit: dense, pyramidal to rounded, deciduous tree **Height:** 20–65' **Spread:** 15–50'
Hardiness: zones 3–8

Magnolia
Magnolia

M. x soulangeana (above & below)

Magnolias are beautiful, fragrant, versatile plants that also provide attractive winter structure.

Growing

Magnolias grow well in **full sun** or **partial shade**. The soil should be **fertile, humus rich, acidic, moist** and **well drained**. A summer mulch helps keep the roots cool and the soil moist.

Tips

Many magnolias are used as specimen trees. The small species can be used in borders.

Avoid planting magnolias where the morning sun will encourage the blooms to open too early in the season. Cold, wind and rain can damage the blossoms.

Recommended

Many species, hybrids and cultivars, in a range of sizes and with differing flowering times and flower colors, are available. Two of the most common ones are given below. Check with your local nursery or garden center for other available magnolias.

*M. x **soulangeana*** (saucer magnolia) is a rounded, spreading, deciduous shrub or tree with pink, purple or white flowers.

*M. **stellata*** (star magnolia) is a compact, bushy or spreading, deciduous shrub or small tree with fragrant, many-petaled, white flowers.

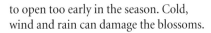

Features: attractive, possibly fragrant, pink, white or purple flowers; fruit; leathery foliage; attractive bark **Habit:** upright to spreading, deciduous shrub or tree **Height:** 8–40' **Spread:** 5–35' **Hardiness:** zones 3–9

Maple
Acer

Maples are attractive year-round, with delicate flowers in spring, attractive foliage and hanging samaras in summer, vibrant leaf color in fall and interesting bark and branch structures in winter.

Growing

Most species of maples do well in **full sun** or **light shade**. The soil should be **fertile, moist, high in organic matter** and **well drained**.

Tips

Maples can be used as specimen trees, as large elements in shrub or mixed borders or as hedges. Some are useful as understory plants bordering wooded areas; others can be grown in containers on patios or terraces. Most Japanese gardens showcase the attractive smaller species. Almost all maples can be used to create bonsai specimens.

A. palmatum cultivars (above & below)

Recommended

Some of the most popular trees used for shade or street plantings are maples. Many are very large when fully mature, but small species useful for small gardens include **A. campestre** (hedge maple), **A. ginnala** (amur maple), **A. griseum** (paperbark maple), **A. palmatum** (Japanese maple) and **A. rubrum** (red maple). Check with your local nursery or garden center for availability.

Features: attractive foliage, bark and form; fall color; red or green flowers; winged fruit
Habit: single or multi-stemmed, deciduous tree or large shrub Height: 6–60'
Spread: 6–50' Hardiness: zones 2–8

Oak

Quercus

Q. robur (above & below)

The typical oak's classic shape, outstanding fall color, deep roots and long life are some of its many assets. Plant one for your own enjoyment and for posterity.

Growing

Oaks grow well in **full sun** or **partial shade**. The soil should be **fertile, moist** and **well drained**. These trees can be difficult to establish, so transplant them only when young.

Tips

These large trees are best as specimens or for groves in parks and large gardens.

Do not disturb the ground around the base of an oak, because oaks are very sensitive to changes in grade.

Recommended

There are many oaks to choose from. Check with your local nursery or garden center. Here are few popular species. Some cultivars are available.

Q. alba (white oak) is a rounded, spreading tree with peeling bark and purple-red fall color.

Q. coccinea (scarlet oak) is noted for having the most brilliant red fall color of all the oaks.

Q. robur (English oak) is a rounded, spreading tree with golden yellow fall color.

Q. rubra (red oak) is a rounded, spreading tree with fall color ranging from yellow to red-brown.

Features: attractive summer and fall foliage; interesting bark; acorns **Habit:** large, rounded, spreading, deciduous tree **Height:** 35–120' **Spread:** 10–100' **Hardiness:** zones 3–9

Pine
Pinus

P. mugo (above), *P. strobus* (below)

Pines offer exciting possibilities for any garden. Exotic-looking pines are available with soft or stiff needles, needles with yellow bands, trunks with patterned or mother-of-pearl-like bark and varied forms.

Growing

Pines grow best in **full sun**. These trees adapt to most **well-drained** soils but do not tolerate polluted urban conditions.

Tips

Pines can be used as specimen trees, as hedges or to create windbreaks. Small cultivars can be included in shrub or mixed borders. These trees are not heavy feeders, and fertilizing will encourage rapid new growth that is weak and susceptible to pest and disease problems.

Recommended

The many pine selections range from stately trees to shrubby dwarfs. Check with your local garden center or nursery to find out what is available.

The Austrian pine, P. nigra, has been recommended as the most urban-tolerant pine, but overplanting has led to severe disease problems, some of which can kill a tree in a single growing season.

Features: attractive foliage; sometimes-colorful bark; cones **Habit:** upright, columnar or spreading, evergreen tree **Height:** 2–120' **Spread:** 2–60' **Hardiness:** zones 2–8

Potentilla
Potentilla

P. fruticosa (above & below)

Potentilla is a fuss-free shrub that blooms madly all summer. The cheery, yellow-flowered variety is often seen, but cultivars with flowers in shades of pink, red, orange or white have broadened the use of this reliable shrub.

Growing

Potentilla prefers **full sun** but tolerates partial or light shade. The soil should, preferably, be of **poor to average fertility** and **well drained**. This plant tolerates most conditions, including sandy or clay soil and wet or dry conditions. When established, it tolerates drought. Too much fertilizer or too rich a soil will encourage weak, floppy, disease-prone growth.

Tips

Potentilla is useful in a shrub or mixed border. The small cultivars can be included in rock gardens or on rock walls. On steep slopes, potentilla can prevent soil erosion and reduce lawn maintenance. Potentilla can even be used to form a low informal hedge.

Hot weather or direct sunlight is less likely to affect yellow or white flowers, but orange, red or pink ones may fade until cooler fall weather arrives. Consider planting cultivars with these colors in a lightly or partially shaded location.

Recommended

P. fruticosa has many cultivars. The following are a few of the most popular and interesting. **'Abbotswood'** is one of the best white-flowered cultivars. **'Goldfinger'** has bright yellow flowers. **'Pink Beauty'** bears semi-double, pink flowers. **'Tangerine'** has orange flowers. **'Yellow Gem'** has bright yellow flowers.

Also called: shrubby cinquefoil
Features: attractive yellow, white, pink, orange or red flowers; lobed foliage **Habit:** mounding, deciduous shrub **Height:** 12–60"
Spread: 12–60" **Hardiness:** zones 2–8

Redbud

Cercis

Redbud is an outstanding treasure of spring. Deep magenta flowers bloom before the leaves emerge, and their impact is intense. As the buds open, the flowers turn pink, covering the long, thin branches in vibrant clouds.

Growing

Redbud will grow well in **full sun, partial shade** or **light shade**. The soil should be a **fertile, deep loam** that is **moist** and **well drained**. An understory tree in the forest, it appreciates protection from sweeping winds. With its tender roots, it does not like being transplanted.

Tips

Redbud can be used as a specimen tree, in a shrub or mixed border or in a woodland garden.

Recommended

C. canadensis (eastern redbud) is a spreading, multi-stemmed tree that bears red, purple or pink flowers. Bronze when young, the foliage fades to green over summer and turns bright yellow in fall. Many beautiful cultivars are available.

C. canadensis (above & below)

Redbud is not as long-lived as many other trees, so use its delicate beauty to complement more permanent trees.

Features: attractive spring flowers and fall foliage **Habit:** rounded or spreading, multi-stemmed, deciduous tree or shrub **Height:** 20–30' **Spread:** 25–35' **Hardiness:** zones 4–9

Serviceberry

Amelanchier

A. canadensis (above)

The *Amelanchier* species are first-rate North American natives that bear lacy, white flowers in spring, followed by edible berries. In fall, the foliage color ranges from a glowing apricot to vibrant red.

With a similar but generally sweeter flavor, serviceberry fruit can be used in place of blueberries in any recipe.

Growing

Serviceberries grow well in **full sun** or **light shade**. They prefer **acidic soil** that is **fertile, humus rich, moist** and **well drained** but tolerate some drought once established.

Tips

With spring flowers, edible fruit, attractive leaves that turn red in fall and their often-artistic branch growth, serviceberries make beautiful specimen plants or even shade trees in small gardens. The shrubbier forms can be grown along the edges of a woodland or in a border. Often found growing near water in the wild, serviceberries are beautiful beside ponds or streams.

Recommended

Several species and hybrids are available. A few popular ones are listed below. All three have white flowers, purple fruit and good fall color.

A. **arborea** (downy serviceberry, Juneberry) is a small, single- or multi-stemmed tree.

A. **canadensis** (shadblow serviceberry) is a large, upright, suckering shrub.

A. **x** *grandiflora* (apple serviceberry) is a small, spreading, often multi-stemmed tree.

Also called: saskatoon, juneberry
Features: attractive white spring or early-summer flowers; edible fruit; fall color; smooth, purple-gray bark **Habit:** single- or multi-stemmed, deciduous, large shrub or small tree **Height:** 4–30' **Spread:** 4–30'
Hardiness: zones 3–9

Seven-Son Flower

Heptacodium

*A*s a smallish tree with fragrant, white, September flowers followed by decorative red sepals and fruit, seven-son flower makes a welcome addition to our plant palette.

Growing

Seven-son flower prefers **full sun** but tolerates partial shade. The soil should ideally be of **average fertility, moist** and **well drained,** although this plant is fairly tolerant of most soil conditions, including dry and acidic soil.

Tips

This shrubby tree can be used in place of a shade tree on a small property. Planted near a patio or deck, it will provide light shade, and its fragrant flowers can be enjoyed in late summer. In a border it provides light shade to plants growing below it, and the dark green leaves make a good backdrop for bright perennial and annual flowers.

Seven-son flower's tolerance of salty soils makes it useful where salty snow from walkways is shoveled in winter.

Recommended

H. miconioides is a large, multi-stemmed shrub or small tree with peeling tan bark. In fall, the dark green leaves may become tinged with purple. The clusters of fragrant, creamy white flowers have persistent sepals that turn dark pink to bright red in mid- to late fall and surround small, purple-red fruit.

H. miconioides (above & below)

A fairly recent introduction to North American gardens, seven-son flower may not be available at all garden centers.

Features: attractive bark; fragrant, white, fall flowers; fruit **Habit:** upright to spreading, multi-stemmed, deciduous shrub or small tree **Height:** 15–20' **Spread:** 8–15' **Hardiness:** zones 5–8

Smokebush
Cotinus

Bright fall color, adaptability, flowers of differing colors and overall variable sizes and forms make smokebush and all its cultivars excellent additions to the garden.

Growing
Smokebush grows well in **full sun** or **partial shade**. It prefers soil of **average fertility** that is **moist** and **well drained,** but it adapts to all but very wet soils.

Tips
Smokebush can be used in a shrub or mixed border, as a single specimen or in groups. It is a good choice for a rocky hillside planting.

Recommended
C. coggygria is a bushy, rounded shrub that develops large, puffy plumes of flowers that start out green and gradually turn a pinky gray. The green foliage turns red, orange and yellow in fall. Many cultivars are available, including purple-leaved ones.

C. obovatus (American smoketree) is a small, shrubby understory tree that has spectacular fall color and attractive gray bark. Not easy to find, but worth the effort.

C. coggygria 'Royal Purple' (above)
C. coggygria (below)

Try encouraging a clematis vine to wind its way through the spreading branches of a smokebush.

Also called: smoketree **Features:** attractive green to pink-gray early-summer flowers; summer and fall foliage **Habit:** bushy, rounded, spreading, deciduous tree or shrub **Height:** 10–15' **Spread:** 10–15' **Hardiness:** zones 4–8

Spicebush
Lindera

Named for the spicy scent of the stems when bruised, this native shrub deserves to be more widely used in our gardens.

Growing
Spicebush grows best in **light or partial shade** but tolerates full sun. The soil should be **fertile, moist, acidic** and **well drained**.

Tips
In shaded locations, spicebush can be quite relaxed and open, but it becomes denser in habit the sunnier the location. This plant makes a lovely addition to moist, open woodland gardens in spots where the tiny, but plentiful, greenish yellow flowers can be enjoyed in early spring.

Recommended
L. benzoin is a rounded, dense to open, multi-stemmed, deciduous shrub. Mid-spring's greenish yellow flowers are followed by red berries in summer. The fragrant, dark green foliage turns an incandescent yellow in fall.

L. benzoin (above & below)

The scarlet fruit of spicebush is one of the few berries that can supply necessary fat to migrating and overwintering birds.

Features: fragrant stems and leaves; greenish yellow mid-spring flowers; fall color **Habit:** rounded, dense to open, multi-stemmed, deciduous shrub **Height:** 6–12' **Spread:** 6–12' **Hardiness:** zones 4–9

Spirea
Spiraea

S. x *bumalda* cultivar (above), *S.* x *vanhouttei* (below)

Spireas, seen in so many gardens and with dozens of cultivars, remain undeniable favorites. With a wide range of forms, sizes and colors of both foliage and flowers, spireas have many possible landscape uses.

Growing

Spireas prefer **full sun**. The soil should be **fertile, acidic, moist** and **well drained**. To help prevent foliage burn, provide protection from very hot sun.

Tips

Spireas are used in shrub or mixed borders, in rock gardens and as informal screens and hedges.

Recommended

Many species and cultivars of spirea are available. Here are two popular hybrid groups.

S. x *bumalda* (*S. japonica* 'Bumalda') is a low, broad, mounded shrub with pink flowers. The many cultivars, which have brightly colored foliage, are preferred.

S. x *vanhouttei* (bridal wreath spirea, Vanhoutte spirea) is a dense, bushy shrub with arching branches that bears clusters of white flowers. Check at your local nursery or garden center to see what selections are available.

Features: attractive summer flowers; mounding or arching habit **Habit:** round, bushy, deciduous shrub **Height:** 1–10'
Spread: 1–12' **Hardiness:** zones 3–9

Spruce
Picea

P. abies 'Nidiformis' (above), *P. pungens* var. *glauca* 'Moerheim' (below)

Spruces are among the most commonly grown and commonly abused evergreens. Grow spruces where they have enough room to spread, then let them branch all the way to the ground.

Growing

Spruce trees grow best in **full sun**. The soil should be **deep, moist, well drained** and **neutral to acidic**. These trees generally do not like hot, dry or polluted conditions. Spruces are best grown from small, young stock, because older plants dislike being transplanted.

Tips

Spruces are often used as specimen trees. The dwarf and slow-growing cultivars can also be used in shrub or mixed borders. These trees look most attractive when allowed to keep their lower branches.

Recommended

Spruce are generally upright, pyramidal trees, but cultivars may be low-growing, wide-spreading or even weeping in habit. *P. abies* (Norway spruce), *P. glauca* (white spruce), *P. omorika* (Serbian spruce), *P. orientalis* (Oriental spruce), *P. pungens* (Colorado spruce) and their cultivars are popular and commonly available.

Oil-based pesticides such as dormant oil can take the blue out of your blue-needled spruces. However, the new growth will have the blue coloring

Features: attractive foliage; cones
Habit: conical or columnar, evergreen tree or shrub **Height:** 2–80' **Spread:** 2–25'
Hardiness: zones 2–8

Summersweet Clethra
Clethra

Summersweet clethra attracts butterflies and other pollinators, and is one of the best shrubs for adding fragrance to your garden.

Growing
Summersweet clethra grows best in **light or partial shade**. The soil should be **fertile, humus rich, acidic, moist** and **well drained**.

Tips
Although not an aggressive spreader, this shrub tends to sucker, forming a colony of stems. Use it in a lightly shaded border or in a woodland garden.

When it is young and succulent, you will need to protect it from browsing deer and rabbits.

Recommended
C. alnifolia is a large, rounded, upright, colony-forming shrub. It bears attractive spikes of white flowers in mid- to late summer. The foliage turns yellow in fall. Several cultivars are available, including pink-flowered ones.

C. alnifolia 'Paniculata' (above & below)

Summersweet clethra is useful in damp, shaded gardens, where the late-season flowers are much appreciated.

Also called: sweet pepperbush, sweetspire
Features: fragrant summer flowers; attractive habit; colorful fall foliage **Habit:** rounded, suckering, deciduous shrub **Height:** 2–8'
Spread: 3–8' **Hardiness:** zones 3–9

Viburnum
Viburnum

Good fall color, attractive form, shade tolerance, scented flowers and attractive fruit put the viburnums in a class by themselves.

Growing
Viburnums grow well in **full sun, partial shade** or **light shade**. The soil should be of **average fertility, moist** and **well drained**. Viburnums tolerate both alkaline and acidic soils.

These plants look neatest if deadheaded, but this practice will, of course, prevent fruits from forming. Fruiting is better when more than one plant of a species or cultivar is grown.

Tips
Viburnums can be used in borders and woodland gardens. They are a good choice for plantings near swimming pools.

Recommended
Many viburnum species, hybrids and cultivars are available. Here are a few popular ones.

V. carlesii (Korean spice viburnum) is a dense, bushy, rounded, deciduous shrub with spicy-scented, white or pink flowers (Zones 5–8)

V. dentatum (arrowwood viburnum) is a rounded shrub with scarlet to purple fall color and blue-black fruit (Zones 3–8)

V. opulus (European cranberrybush, Guelder-rose) is a rounded, spreading, deciduous shrub with lacy-looking

V. opulus (above)
V. plicatum var. tomentosum (below)

flower clusters and fruit that ripens to red. (Zones 3–8)

V. plicatum var. *tomentosum* (double-file viburnum) has a graceful horizontal branching pattern that gives the shrub a layered effect. It bears lacy-looking, white flower clusters followed by red fruit. (Zones 5–8)

V. trilobum (American cranberrybush, highbush cranberry) is a dense, rounded shrub with clusters of white flowers followed by edible red fruit. (Zones 2–7)

Features: attractive, possibly fragrant flowers; summer and fall foliage; fruit **Habit:** bushy or spreading, evergreen, semi-evergreen or deciduous shrub **Height:** 18"–20' **Spread:** 18"–15' **Hardiness:** zones 2–8

Weigela
Weigela

W. f. 'Polka' (above),
W. f. 'Siebold Variegata'
(center), *W. florida*
culivar (below)

Weigela has been improved through breeding, and specimens with more compact forms, longer flowering periods and greater cold tolerance are now available.

Growing
Weigela prefers **full sun** but tolerates partial shade. The soil should be **fertile** and **well drained**. This plant adapts to most well-drained soils.

Tips
Weigela can be used in shrub or mixed borders, in open woodland gardens and for informal barrier plantings.

Recommended
W. florida is a spreading shrub with arching branches that bear clusters of dark pink flowers. Many hybrids and cultivars are available, including dwarf varieties and varieties with red, pink or white flowers or with purple, bronze or yellow foliage.

Weigela is one of the longest-blooming shrubs, with the main flush of blooms lasting as long as six weeks. It often re-blooms if sheared lightly after the first flowers fade.

Features: attractive late-spring to early-summer flowers, foliage **Habit:** upright or low, spreading, deciduous shrubs **Height:** 1–9' **Spread:** 1–12' **Hardiness:** zones 3–8

White Cedar
Thuja

White cedars are rot resistant, durable and long-lived, earning quiet admiration from gardeners everywhere.

Growing

White cedars prefer **full sun** but tolerate light to partial shade. The soil should be of **average fertility, moist** and **well drained**. These plants enjoy humidity and in the wild are often found growing near marshy areas. White cedars perform best with some shelter from wind, especially in winter, when the foliage can easily dry out and give the entire plant a rather brown, drab appearance.

Tips

Large varieties of white cedar make excellent specimen trees, and smaller cultivars can be used in foundation plantings and shrub borders and as formal or informal hedges.

Recommended

T. occidentalis (eastern arborvitae, eastern white cedar) is a narrow, pyramidal tree with scale-like, evergreen needles. Dozens of cultivars are available, including smaller upright varieties, varieties with yellow foliage and shrubby or

T. occidentalis 'Little Gem' with boxwoods (above)
T. occidentalis (below)

upright dwarf varieties. (Zones 2–7; cultivars may be less cold hardy)

T. plicata (western arborvitae, western red cedar) is a narrowly pyramidal evergreen tree that grows quickly, resists deer browsing and maintains good foliage color all winter. Several cultivars are available, including several dwarf varieties and a variegated, yellow-and-green variety. (Zones 5–9)

Also called: arborvitae **Features:** attractive foliage, habit and bark **Habit:** small to large, evergreen shrub or tree **Height:** 2–50' **Spread:** 2–20' **Hardiness:** zones 2–8

Witchhazel

Hamamelis

H. virginiana (above & below)

Witchhazels are an investment in happiness. The early-spring flowers of vernal witchhazel last for weeks, and their spicy fragrance awakens the senses. Then, in fall, the handsome leaves develop overlapping bands of orange, yellow and red.

Growing

Witchhazels grow best in a sheltered spot with **full sun** or **light shade**. The soil should be of **average fertility, neutral to acidic, moist** and **well drained**.

Tips

Witchhazels work well individually or in groups. They can be used as specimen plants, in shrub or mixed borders and in woodland gardens. As small trees, they are ideal for space-limited gardens.

The unique flowers have long, narrow, crinkled petals that give the blooming plant a spidery appearance. If the weather gets too cold, the petals will roll up, protecting the flowers and extending the flowering season.

Recommended

H. x *intermedia* is a vase-shaped, spreading shrub that bears fragrant flower clusters in shades of yellow, orange or red. The leaves turn attractive shades of orange, red and bronze in fall.

H. vernalis (vernal witchhazel) and *H. virginiana* (common witchhazel) are our native witchhazels; they produce yellow flowers in early spring and late fall respectively. The vernal typically grows one-third as big as common witchhazel. Both are shrubs or small trees.

Features: fragrant early-spring flowers; attractive summer and fall foliage **Habit**: spreading, deciduous shrub or small tree **Height**: 6–30' **Spread**: 6–30' **Hardiness**: zones 5–8

Yew

Taxus

From sweeping hedges to commanding specimens, yews can serve many purposes in the garden. Although some other evergreens tolerate or prefer some shade, yews are the only reliable choice for deep shade.

Growing

Yews grow well in any light conditions from **full sun to full shade**. The soil should be **fertile, moist** and **well drained**. These trees tolerate windy, dry and polluted conditions and soils of any acidity. They dislike excessive heat, however, and in a hot location on the south or southwest side of a building they may suffer needle scorch.

Tips

Yews can be used in borders or as specimens, hedges, topiary and groundcovers.

Male and female flowers are borne on separate plants. Both must be present to produce the attractive red seed cups.

T. x media 'Fairview' (above), *T. x media* cultivar (below)

Recommended

T. x media (English Japanese yew), a cross between *T. baccata* (English yew) and *T. cuspidata* (Japanese yew), has the vigor of the English yew and the cold hardiness of the Japanese yew. The many cultivars form rounded, upright trees or shrubs of varying sizes and forms.

Features: attractive foliage; red seed cups
Habit: evergreen; conical or columnar tree or bushy or spreading shrub **Height:** 1–70'
Spread: 1–30' **Hardiness:** zones 4–7

Apothecary's Rose

Species Rose

R. glauca 'Officinalis (above & below)

Apothecary's Rose is known for its culinary and medicinal value and its use in crafts, particularly in potpourri.

This rose has been cultivated since the 13th century, and it was used in herbal medicine to treat inflammation, aches, pains and insomnia.

Growing

Apothecary's Rose prefers **full sun** but tolerates afternoon shade. The soil should be **average to fertile, slightly acidic, humus rich, moist** and **well drained**. The suckers it produces should be removed once flowering is complete.

Tips

Apothecary's Rose can be grown as a specimen, in a shrub border or as a hedge. It can be naturalized or used to prevent soil erosion on a bank too steep for mowing. The flowers are very fragrant; plant this shrub near windows, doors and frequently used pathways.

Recommended

Rosa gallica **'Officinalis'** is a bushy, rounded, vigorous, disease-resistant shrub with bristly stems and dark green leaves. One flush of semi-double flowers is produced each year in late spring or early summer. *Rosa gallica* **'Versicolor'** has white or light pink flowers with darker pink splashes and stripes.

Also called: red damask, red rose of Lancaster
Features: rounded habit; fresh and intensely fragrant early-summer flowers in crimson purple or pinkish red; dark red hips **Height:** 30"–4'
Spread: 30"–4' **Hardiness:** zones 4–10

Carefree Delight

Modern Shrub Rose

R. 'Carefree Delight' (above & below)

The name of this shrub rose is perfectly appropriate—it requires very little care and produces copious quantities of flowers in waves throughout summer.

Growing

Carefree Delight prefers **full sun** but tolerates some shade. The soil should be **average to fertile, humus rich, slightly acidic, moist** and **well drained,** but this rose has proven to be quite adaptable to a variety of soil conditions. Carefree Delight is disease resistant.

Tips

Carefree Delight makes a good addition to a mixed bed or border. Equally attractive as a specimen or in groups, it can be mass planted to create a large display.

Recommended

Rosa 'Carefree Delight' is a bushy, rounded shrub with glossy, dark green foliage that turns bronzy red in fall. Large clusters of pink, single flowers with white or yellow centers and contrasting yellow stamens are borne for most of summer. Other roses in the 'Carefree' series include **'Carefree Beauty,'** with medium pink, double flowers, and **'Carefree Sunshine,'** with yellow flowers.

Features: rounded habit; summer and fall foliage; long blooming period; single or double flowers in yellow or pink with white or yellow centers; attractive hips; disease resistant
Height: 3–4' **Spread:** 3–4'
Hardiness: zones 4–9

Fair Bianca

English or Austin Rose

David Austin roses are famous for the fragrance of their flowers. Fair Bianca has lovely white flowers with a spicy scent.

Growing
Fair Bianca, like all Austin roses, grows best in **full sun** in a **warm, sheltered** location. The soil should be **fertile, humus rich, slightly acidic, moist** and **well drained**. Deadhead to keep plants tidy and encourage continuous blooming.

Tips
Austin roses such as Fair Bianca make good additions to mixed beds and borders. They are equally attractive as specimens or when planted in groups and can be mass planted to create a large display.

Recommended
Rosa 'Fair Bianca' forms a rounded shrub with light green foliage. The very double flowers are borne in clusters and may be white, buff or very pale yellow.

Other Austin roses are available. They include 'Golden Celebration,' with yellow flowers; 'Eglantyne,' with pink flowers; 'Pat Austin,' with orange flowers; and 'Evelyn,' with apricot flowers.

Features: rounded habit; long blooming period; fragrant, white to pale yellow flowers
Height: 30–42" **Spread:** 2–3'
Hardiness: zones 4–9

Fourth Of July
Climbing Rose

W hen Fourth of July was named an All-American Rose Selection in 1999, more than 20 years had passed since a climbing rose had won this prestigious honor.

Growing
Fourth of July prefers **full sun** but tolerates partial shade. The soil should be **average to fertile, humus rich, slightly acidic, moist** and **well drained.** This rose is disease resistant.

Tips
Train Fourth of July to climb arbors, trellises and fences. With some judicious pruning, this rose can be trained to form a bushy shrub. Plant this rose where the summer-long profusion of blooms will welcome visitors to your home.

Recommended
Rosa **'Fourth of July'** is a vigorous shrub with long, arching stems. The clusters of ruffled flowers with red, pink and white stripes contrast nicely with the dark green foliage.

Fourth of July blooms differ from flower to flower, displaying varied combinations of stripes and speckles.

Also called: Crazy for You, Hanabi
Features: climbing habit; glossy, green foliage; apple-scented, ruffled, multi-colored flowers of red, pink and white; long blooming period **Height:** 8–10' **Spread:** 3–6'
Hardiness: zones 4–9

Golden Wings

Modern Shrub Rose

Since its 1956 introduction, Golden Wings has set the standard for single-flowered shrub roses with yellow flowers.

Growing

Golden Wings prefers **full sun** but tolerates some shade. The soil should be **average to fertile, humus rich, slightly acidic, moist** and **well drained,** but this rose has proven to be quite adaptable to a variety of soil conditions, including poor, less fertile soils. Golden Wings is disease resistant unless grown in very stressful conditions. Deadhead for best repeat blooming.

Tips

Golden Wings looks good and grows well with other plants, and it can be included in a shrub or mixed border as a specimen or planted in groups. It is also suitable to use as a hedge. The flowers stand up well to harsh weather, and the plants are quite cold hardy.

Recommended

Rosa 'Golden Wings' is a bushy, rounded shrub with pale green leaves and clusters of single, light yellow flowers. It begins flowering earlier in the season than most other shrub roses and continues to bloom repeatedly all summer. The large, very round hips eventually turn orange or reddish.

Golden Wings is a living tribute to its creator, Roy Shepherd, a famous rosarian who died in 1962.

Features: bushy, rounded habit; light green foliage; delicate, orange- and honey-scented, light yellow flowers; long blooming period
Height: 4–5' **Spread:** 4'
Hardiness: zones 4–9

Gourmet Popcorn

Miniature Rose

Gourmet Popcorn bears cascading clusters of honey-scented, rounded, white, semi-double flowers with short stems.

Growing

Gourmet Popcorn prefers **full sun**. The soil should be **fertile, humus rich, moist** and **well drained**. It tolerates light breezes but dislikes strong winds.

Tips

Gourmet Popcorn looks stunning planted en masse or in pots, containers or hanging baskets. Plant this rose where its fragrance can be enjoyed—alongside pathways, under windows or next to a garden bench or seat.

Recommended

Rosa '**Gourmet Popcorn**' is a vigorous, compact, cushion-like, rounded shrub with lush, dark green foliage. It is resistant to disease.

In warmer regions, Gourmet Popcorn can grow to twice the typical height, creating an impressive specimen with hundreds of flowers in bloom at a time.

Also called: Summer Snow
Features: rounded habit; repeat blooming of abundant, white flowers from summer to fall   **Height:** 18–24" **Spread:** 24"
Hardiness: zones 4–9

Hansa

Rugosa Shrub Rose

Hansa, first introduced in 1905, is one of the most durable, long-lived and versatile roses.

Growing

Hansa grows best in **full sun.** The soil should preferably be **average to fertile, humus rich, slightly acidic, moist** and **well drained,** but this durable rose adapts to most soils, from sandy soil to silty clay. Remove a few of the oldest canes every few years to keep the plants blooming vigorously.

Hansa is derived from Rosa rugosa, *a wide-spreading plant with disease-resistant foliage that is also found in many of its hybrids and cultivars.*

Tips

Rugosa roses such as Hansa make good additions to mixed borders and beds, and they can also be used as hedges or as specimens. They are often used on steep banks to prevent soil erosion. Their prickly branches deter people from walking across flower beds and compacting the soil.

Recommended

Rosa 'Hansa' is a bushy shrub with arching canes and leathery, deeply veined, bright green leaves. The double flowers are produced all summer. The bright orange hips persist past the end of fall. Another rugosa rose, **'Blanc Double de Coubert,'** produces white, double flowers all summer.

Features: dense, arching habit; clove-scented, mauve purple or mauve red flowers from early summer to fall; orange-red hips **Height:** 4–5'
Spread: 5–6'
Hardiness: zones 3–9

Knockout

Modern Shrub Rose

This rose is simply one of the best new shrub roses to hit the market in years. It graces the garden with a good rose fragrance combined with exceptional disease resistance.

Growing

Knockout grows best in **full sun**. The soil should be **fertile, humus rich, slightly acidic, moist** and **well drained**. Blooming is most prolific in warm weather, but the flowers are a deeper red in cooler weather. Deadhead lightly to keep the plant tidy and to encourage prolific blooming.

Tips

This vigorous, attractive rose makes a good addition to a mixed bed or border. Equally attractive as a specimen or in groups, it can be mass planted to create a large display.

Recommended

Rosa 'Knockout' has a lovely rounded form with glossy, green leaves that turn to shades of burgundy in fall. The bright cherry red flowers are borne in clusters of 3–15 almost all summer and in early fall. The orange-red hips last well beyond fall. **'Double Knockout'**, **'Pink Knockout'** and a light pink selection called **'Blushing Knockout'** are also available. All have excellent disease resistance.

If you've been afraid that roses need too much care, you'll appreciate the hardiness and disease resistance of this low-maintenance beauty.

Also called: Knock Out
Features: rounded habit; cherry red flowers with light tea rose scent from mid-summer to fall; disease resistant **Height:** 3–4'
Spread: 3–4' **Hardiness:** zones 4–10

New Dawn
Climbing Rose

Introduced in 1930, New Dawn, a sport of Dr. van Fleet, is still a favorite climbing rose of gardeners and rosarians alike.

Growing
New Dawn grows best in **full sun**. The soil should be **average to fertile, humus** rich, **slightly acidic, moist** and **well drained**. This rose is disease resistant.

Tips
Train New Dawn to climb pergolas, walls, pillars, arbors, trellises and fences. With some judicious pruning, this rose can be trained to form a bushy shrub or hedge. Plant this rose where the summer-long profusion of blooms will welcome visitors to your home.

Recommended
Rosa **'New Dawn'** is a vigorous climber with upright, arching canes and glossy, green foliage. It bears pale pink flowers, singly or in small clusters.

New Dawn was inducted into the World Federation of Rose Societies' Hall of Fame in 1997.

Features: glossy, green foliage; climbing habit; long blooming period; pale pearl pink flowers with sweet, apple-like fragrance
Height: 10–15' **Spread:** 10–15'
Hardiness: zones 4–9

Rosa glauca
Species Rose

This species rose is a gardener's dream—it's hardy, has good disease resistance and bears striking foliage in summer and colorful hips in winter.

Growing

Rosa glauca grows best and develops contrasting foliage color in **full sun** but tolerates some shade. The soil should be **average to fertile, humus rich, slightly acidic, moist** and **well drained,** but this rose adapts to most soils, from sandy soil to silty clay.

Remove a few of the oldest canes to the ground every few years to encourage younger, more colorful stems to grow in. Leave the spent flowers to develop into hips— removing them won't prolong the blooming period.

Tips

With its unusual foliage color, *Rosa glauca* makes a good addition to mixed borders and beds, and it can also be used as a hedge or specimen.

Recommended

Rosa glauca (*R. rubrifolia*) is a bushy shrub with arching, purple-tinged canes and delicate, purple-tinged, blue-green leaves. The single, star-like flowers bloom in clusters in late spring. The dark red hips persist until spring.

Because of its hardiness, disease resistance, dainty blooms and foliage color, Rosa glauca *is extremely popular with rosarians and novice gardeners alike. It received the Royal Horticultural Society's Award of Garden Merit—proof of its dependable performance.*

Also called: red-leaved rose
Features: dense, arching habit; purple- or red-tinged foliage; late-spring flowers of mauve pink with white centers; persistent, dark red hips **Height:** 6–10' **Spread:** 5–6'
Hardiness: zones 2–9

Rose de Rescht

Old Garden Rose

*I*ts heady scent, densely petaled flowers and long blooming period make this old-fashioned Damask rose a perpetual favorite.

Growing
Rose de Rescht grows best in **full sun.** The soil should preferably be **average to fertile, humus rich, slightly acidic, moist** and **well drained,** but this durable rose adapts to most soils and conditions.

Tips
Use Rose de Rescht in a mixed or shrub border. It can be planted as a specimen or in groups. Plant it where you can enjoy the heady scent of the flowers.

Recommended
Rosa **'Rose de Rescht'** is a dense, bushy shrub with dark green foliage. The richly scented, double, purple to reddish flowers are produced in clusters from mid-summer to fall; they may pale slightly during hot weather.

Although the origin of Rose de Rescht is uncertain, it became popular after plant collector and writer Nancy Lindsay found it in Rescht, Iran, in 1945 and brought it to England.

Features: bushy habit; dark green foliage; fragrant, deep vibrant purple or fuchsia red flowers; long blooming period **Height:** 30–42" **Spread:** 2–3' **Hardiness:** zones 4–9

Wild Spice

Rugosa Shrub Rose

Wild Spice is the "new kid on the block" in the Rugosa group. Often considered to be a somewhat petite rose, in good soil it can reach higher than described below.

Growing

Wild Spice grows best in **full sun**. The soil should preferably be **average to fertile, humus rich, slightly acidic, moist** and **well drained,** but this durable rose adapts to most soils. Remove a few of the oldest canes every few years to keep the plants blooming vigorously.

Tips

Rugosa roses such as Wild Spice make good additions to mixed borders and beds, and they can also be used as hedges or as specimens. They are often used on steep banks to prevent soil erosion. Their prickly branches deter people from walking across flower beds and compacting the soil.

Recommended

Rosa 'Wild Spice' is a bushy shrub with arching canes and leathery, deeply veined, dark green leaves. The snowy white, delicately ruffled, single flowers are produced in small clusters all summer. The bright orange hips persist beyond fall.

Low-maintenance roses are a must for the busy gardener. Wild Spice has some of the best features that roses can offer: along with disease resistance, it offers a long season of fragrant flowers followed by attractive rose hips useful for culinary purposes.

Features: dense, arching habit; clove-scented, white flowers from early summer to fall; orange hips **Height:** 3–4'
Spread: 30"–3' **Hardiness:** zones 5–8

Black-Eyed Susan Vine
Thunbergia

T. alata 'Red Shades' (above), *T. alata* (below)

Black-eyed Susan vine blooms are actually trumpet-shaped; their typically dark centers or 'eyes' form a tube.

Use black-eyed Susan vine to heat up your garden walls with a splash of golden orange. Or, cool down your garden with its cousin, the cool blue skyflower vine.

Growing

Black-eyed Susan vines do well in **full sun, partial shade** or **light shade**. Grow them in **fertile, moist, well-drained** soil that is **high in organic matter**.

Tips

Black-eyed Susan vines can be trained to twine up and around fences, walls, trees and shrubs. They look attractive in mixed containers, window boxes and hanging baskets, or trailing down from the top of a rock garden or rock wall.

Recommended

T. alata (black-eyed Susan vine) is a vigorous, twining climber. It bears deep gold to orange flowers, often with dark centers, in summer and fall. Cultivars with large flowers in yellow, orange or white are available.

T. grandiflora (skyflower vine, blue trumpet vine) is less commonly available than *T. alata*. It tends to bloom late, in early to mid-fall. This twining climber bears stunning, pale violet blue flowers. **'Alba'** has white flowers.

Features: twining habit; yellow, orange, violet blue or creamy white flowers, often with dark centers **Height:** 5' **Spread:** 5' **Hardiness:** tender perennial treated as an annual

Clematis

Clematis

Often called the queen of vines, clematis offers an amazing selection of bloom color. And, if you chose your cultivars wisely, you can have clematis in bloom for most of the season.

Growing

Clematis plants prefer **full sun** but tolerate partial shade. The soil should be **fertile, humus rich, moist** and **well drained**. These vines enjoy warm, sunny weather, but the roots prefer to be cool. A thick layer of mulch or a planting of low, shade-providing perennials protects the tender roots. Many clematis species are quite cold hardy, but they fare best when protected from winter wind. The rootball of a clematis should be planted about 2" beneath the surface of the soil.

Tips

Clematis vines can climb up structures such as trellises, railings, fences and arbors. They can also be allowed to grow over shrubs and up trees or used as groundcover.

Recommended

Clematis species, hybrids and cultivars offer varied flower forms, colors and sizes, blooming times and heights. Some bear scented flowers. Check with your local garden center to see what is available.

C. 'Jackmanii Rubra' (above), *C.* 'Gravetye Beauty' (below)

Plant two clematis varieties that bloom at the same time to provide a mix of color and texture in one spot.

Features: twining habit; possibly scented flowers of blue, purple, pink, yellow, red or white in spring, summer or fall; decorative seedheads **Height:** 10–17' or more **Spread:** 5' or more **Hardiness:** zones 3–8

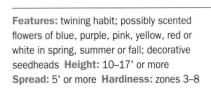

Climbing Hydrangea
Hydrangea

H. anomala subsp. *petiolaris* (above & below)

When mature, a climbing hydrangea can cover an entire wall. With its dark, glossy leaves and delicate, lacy flowers, this vine is quite possibly one of the most stunning climbing plants available.

Growing

Climbing hydrangea prefers **partial or light shade** but tolerates full sun or full shade. The soil should be of **average to**

Climbing hydrangea produces the most flowers when exposed to some direct sunlight each day.

high fertility, humus rich, moist and **well drained**. This plant performs best in cool, moist conditions, so be sure to mulch its roots.

Tips

Climbing hydrangea climbs up trees, walls, fences, pergolas and arbors. Clinging to walls by means of aerial roots, it needs no support, just a somewhat textured surface. It also grows over rocks and can be used as a groundcover or trained to form a small tree or shrub.

Recommended

H. anomala subsp. *petiolaris* (*H. petiolaris*) is a clinging, deciduous vine with glossy, dark green leaves that sometimes turn an attractive yellow in fall. For more than a month in mid-summer, the vine is covered with white, lacy-looking flowers, and the entire plant appears to be veiled in a lacy mist.

Features: white flowers; clinging habit; exfoliating bark **Height:** 50–80'
Spread: 50–80' **Hardiness:** zones 4–9

Cup-and-Saucer Vine

Cobaea

C. scandens (above & below)

Cup-and-saucer vine, a vigorous climber native to Mexico, produces frilly, purple flowers from spring until frost.

Growing

Cup-and-saucer vine prefers **full sun**. The soil should be of **average fertility** and **well drained**. Fond of hot weather, this plant grows best in a sheltered site with southern exposure. When planting the seeds, set them on edge and barely cover them with soil. They take over two weeks to germinate.

Tips

Grow this vine up a trellis, over an arbor or along a chain-link fence. Cup-and-saucer vine grows grabbing hooks to climb and therefore needs a rough-textured support, such as a trellis or coarse-textured wall, to hold onto. It can be trained to fill almost any space. In a hanging basket, the vines will climb the hanger and spill over the edges of the pot.

Recommended

C. scandens is a vigorous climbing vine. The flowers open creamy green and mature to deep purple. For white flowers, try **var. *alba*.**

Also called: cathedral bells
Features: clinging habit; long blooming period; purple or white flowers
Height: 15–25' **Spread:** 15–25'
Hardiness: tender perennial treated as an annual

Hardy Kiwi
Actinidia

A. arguta 'Ananasaya' (above), *A. arguta* (below)

Hardy kiwis are handsome in their simplicity. Their lush green leaves, vigor and adaptability make them very useful, especially on difficult sites.

Growing
Hardy kiwi vines grow best in **full sun**. The soil should be **fertile** and **well drained**. These plants require shelter from strong winds.

Tips
These vines need a sturdy structure to twine around. Pergolas, arbors and sufficiently large and sturdy fences provide

Both a male and a female vine must be present for fruit to be produced. The plants are often sold in pairs.

good support. Given a trellis against a wall, a tree or some other upright structure, hardy kiwis twine upward all summer. They can also be grown in large containers.

Hardy kiwi vines can grow uncontrollably. Don't be afraid to prune them back if they are getting out of hand.

Recommended
Two hardy kiwi vines are commonly grown in cold-climate gardens.

A. **arguta** (hardy kiwi, bower actinidia) has heart-shaped, dark green leaves, white flowers and smooth-skinned, greenish yellow, edible fruit.

A. **kolomikta** (variegated kiwi vine, kolomikta actinidia) has green leaves strongly variegated with pink and white, white flowers and smooth-skinned, greenish yellow, edible fruit.

Features: early-summer flowers; edible fruit; twining habit **Height:** 15–30' to indefinite **Spread:** 15–30' to indefinite **Hardiness:** zones 3–7

Hops
Humulus

*I*f you sit near hops for an afternoon, you might actually be able to watch the plant grow. I have noted 2' of growth in a single day in early summer.

Growing
Hops grow best in **full sun**. The soil should be **average to fertile, humus rich, moist** and **well drained,** but established plants adapt to most conditions if they are well watered for the first few years.

Tips
Hops quickly twine around any sturdy support to create a screen or shade a patio or deck. Provide a pergola, arbor, porch rail or even a telephone pole for hops to grow up. Most trellises are too delicate for this vigorous grower.

Recommended
H. *lupulus* is a fast-growing, twining vine with rough-textured, bright green leaves and stems. The fragrant, cone-like flowers—produced only on the female plants and used to flavor and preserve beer—open pale green and ripen to beige. A cultivar with golden yellow foliage is available.

H. lupulus (above & below)

As true perennials, hops send up new shoots from ground level each year. The previous year's growth needs to be cleared away each fall or spring.

Features: twining habit; dense growth; cone-like, pale green late-summer flowers that ripen to beige **Height:** 10–20' **Spread:** 10–20' **Hardiness:** zones 3–8

Hydrangea Vine

Schizophragma

S. hydrangeoides (above & below)

This vine is similar in appearance to climbing hydrangea, but the dark green leaves have a shimmery, silver sheen that adds another color tone to the garden.

Growing
Hydrangea vine grows well in **full sun** or **partial shade**. The soil should be **average to fertile, humus rich, moist** and **well drained**.

Tips
Hydrangea vine clings to any rough surface and looks attractive climbing a wall, fence, tree, pergola or arbor. It can also be used as a groundcover on a bank or allowed to grow up or over a rock wall.

Because this vine has trouble clinging to a smooth-surfaced wall, attach a few supports to the wall and tie the vines to them—they will eventually be hidden by the dense growth.

Recommended
S. hydrangeoides is an attractive climbing vine that bears lacy clusters of white flowers in mid-summer. **'Moonlight'** has silvery blue foliage. **'Roseum'** bears clusters of pink flowers.

The elegant hydrangea vine adds a touch of glamour to even the most ordinary-looking home.

Also called: Japanese hydrangea vine
Features: clinging habit; dark green and silvery foliage; white or pink flowers
Height: up to 40' **Spread:** up to 40'
Hardiness: zones 5–8

Wisteria
Wisteria

W. sinensis (above & below)

All parts of wisterias, including the seeds in the long, bean-like pods, are poisonous.

Loose clusters of purple flowers hang like lace from the branches of the classic wisteria. A gardener willing to use garden shears can create beautiful tree forms and attractive arbor specimens.

Growing

Wisterias grow well in **full sun** or **partial shade**. The soil should be of **average fertility, moist** and **well drained**. Vines grown in too fertile a soil produce lots of vegetative growth but very few flowers. Avoid planting wisteria near a lawn where fertilizer may leach over to your vine.

Tips

These vines require something to twine around, such as an arbor or other sturdy structure. You can also train a wisteria to form a small tree. Try to select a permanent site; wisterias don't like being moved. These vigorous vines may send up suckers and can root wherever branches touch the ground.

Recommended

W. floribunda (Japanese wisteria) bears long, pendulous clusters of fragrant blue, purple, pink or white flowers in late spring before the leaves emerge. Long, bean-like pods follow.

W. sinensis (Chinese wisteria) bears long, pendant clusters of fragrant, blue-purple flowers in late spring. **'Alba'** has white flowers.

Features: late-spring flowers; foliage; twining habit **Height:** 20–50' or more **Spread:** 20–50' or more **Hardiness:** zones 4–9

Morning Glory
Ipomoea

M orning glories will embellish a chain-link fence, a wire topiary structure or any object thin enough for the tendrils to twine around.

Growing

Morning glories prefer **full sun**. The soil should be of **poor fertility, light** and **well drained,** although the plants adapt to most soils. If sowing indoors, start the seeds in individual peat pots. Soak the seeds for 24 hours prior to sowing. Plant out in late spring.

Tips

Morning glories can be grown anywhere: on fences, walls, trees, trellises or arbors. As groundcovers, they can cover any obstacles they encounter.

In order to climb, these vines must have something small enough to twine around. Wide fence posts, walls and other broad objects must have narrow wire or a trellis attached to them if you want your morning glories to cover them.

Recommended

I. alba (moonflower) has sweetly scented, white flowers that open at night.

I. purpurea (common morning glory) bears trumpet-shaped flowers in purple, blue, pink or white.

I. tricolor (morning glory) produces purple or blue flowers with white centers. Many cultivars are available.

Features: fast growth; white, blue, pink, purple or variegated summer flowers
Height: 10–12' **Spread:** 12–24"
Hardiness: annual

I. alba (above), *I. tricolor* (below)

Each morning glory flower lasts for only one day. The flower bud forms a spiral that slowly unfurls as the day brightens with the rising sun.

Canna Lily

Canna

Canna lilies are stunning, dramatic plants that give an exotic flair to any garden.

Growing

Canna lilies grow best in **full sun** in a **sheltered** location. The soil should be **fertile, moist** and **well drained**. Plant out in spring, once the soil has warmed. Plants can be started early indoors in containers to get a head start on the growing season. Dead-head to prolong blooming.

Tips

Canna lilies can be grown in a bed or border. They make dramatic specimen plants and can even be included in large planters.

Recommended

Canna lily cultivars and hybrids offer a wide range of both tall and dwarf selections, including ones with foliage that is green, bronzy purple or striped in yellow and green. The flowers may be white, red, orange, pink, yellow or bicolored.

C. 'Red King Humbert' (above & below)

Canna lily rhizomes can be lifted after the foliage dies back in fall. Clean off any clinging dirt and store them in a cool, frost-free location in slightly moist peat moss. Check on them regularly through winter; if they start to sprout, pot them and move them to a bright window until they can be moved outdoors.

Features: decorative foliage; white, red, orange, pink, yellow or bicolored summer flowers **Height:** 18"–6' **Spread:** 20–36" **Hardiness:** zones 7–9; usually grown as an annual

Crocus

Crocus

C. x *vernus* cultivars (above & below)

Crocuses are harbingers of spring. They often appear, as if by magic, in full bloom from beneath the melting snow.

Growing

Crocuses grow well in **full sun** or **light, dappled shade**. The soil should be of **poor to average fertility, gritty** and **well drained**. Plant the corms about 4" deep in fall.

Saffron is obtained from the dried, crushed stigmas of C. sativus. *Six plants produce enough spice for one recipe. This fall-blooming plant is hardy to zone 6 and can be grown successfully in the mild parts of Ohio.*

Tips

Crocuses are almost always planted in groups. Drifts of crocuses can be planted in lawns to provide interest and color while the grass still lies dormant. In beds and borders, they can be left to naturalize. Groups of plants will fill in and spread out to provide a bright welcome in spring.

Recommended

Crocus species, hybrids and cultivars offer many choices. The spring-flowering crocus most people are familiar with is **C. x vernus**, commonly called Dutch crocus. Many cultivars are available, with flowers in shades of purple, yellow and white; some are bicolored or have darker veins.

Features: early-spring flowers in purple, yellow, white or bicolored **Height:** 2–6" **Spread:** 2–4" **Hardiness:** zones 3–8

Cyclamen

Cyclamen

C. hederifolium (above & below)

This diminutive plant makes a lovely addition to shade gardens. The attractively patterned foliage and fall flowers in shades of pink or white provide interest in a season dominated by yellows and oranges.

Growing

Cyclamen grows best in **light or partial shade**. The soil should be **fertile, humus-rich** and **well drained**. Add a layer of compost to the soil each spring.

Tips

Cyclamen is an attractive plant to use in shaded beds, borders, rock gardens and woodland gardens. If planted in containers, they may need winter protection because of the greater root temperature fluctuations.

Also called: hardy cyclamen
Features: attractive evergreen foliage; pink or white fall flowers **Height:** 4–6"
Spread: 6–8" **Hardiness:** zones 5–9

Recommended

C. hederifolium forms a low clump of triangular to heart-shaped, evergreen foliage from fall to mid-summer. The dark green foliage is patterned with light green and silvery markings. Pink or white flowers are produced in fall. Plants often go dormant during the heat of summer.

The charming down-facing flowers and the marbled foliage of these beauties are worth waiting the time it takes for cyclamen to spread.

Daffodil

Narcissus

When they think of daffodils, many gardeners automatically picture large, trumpet-shaped, yellow flowers, but daffodils offer a lot of variety in color, form and size.

Growing

Daffodils grow best in **full sun** or **light, dappled shade**. The soil should be **average to fertile, moist** and **well drained**. Plant the bulbs in fall, 2–8" deep, depending on the size of the bulb. As a guide, measure the bulb from top to bottom and multiply that number by three to know how deeply to plant.

Tips

Daffodils are often planted where they can be left to naturalize, in the light shade beneath a tree or in a woodland garden. In mixed beds and borders, the faded leaves are hidden by the summer foliage of other plants.

The cup in the center of a daffodil is the corona, and the group of petals that surrounds the corona is the perianth.

Recommended

Many species, hybrids and cultivars are available. The flowers come in shades of white, yellow, peach, orange, pink or bicolored. Ranging from 1½ to 6" across, they can be solitary or borne in clusters and come in 13 flower form categories.

Features: white, yellow, peach, orange and pink or bicolored spring flowers **Height:** 4–24" **Spread:** 4–12" **Hardiness:** zones 3–9

Dahlia

Dahlia

The variation in size, shape and color of dahlia flowers is astonishing. You are sure to find at least one that appeals to you.

Growing

Dahlias prefer **full sun**. The soil should be **fertile,** rich in **organic matter, moist** and **well drained**. All dahlias are tender, tuberous perennials that are usually treated as annuals. The tubers can be purchased and started early indoors. They can be lifted in fall and stored over winter in slightly moist peat moss. Pot them and keep them in a bright room when they start sprouting in mid- to late winter. Deadhead to keep the plants tidy and blooming.

Tips

Dahlias make attractive, colorful additions to a mixed border. The small varieties make good edging plants, and the large ones make good alternatives to shrubs. Varieties with unusual or interesting flowers make attractive specimen plants.

Recommended

Dahlia hybrids are mostly grown from tubers, but a few can be started from seed. Many hybrids are sold based on flower shape, such as collarette, decorative or peony-flowered. The flowers range in size from 2" to 12" and are available in shades of purple, pink, white, yellow, orange, red or bicolored.

Features: summer flowers in purple, pink, white, yellow, orange, red or bicolored; attractive foliage, bushy habit Height: 8–60" Spread: 8–18" Hardiness: tender perennial; grown as an annual

Check with your local garden center to see what is available.

Dahlia cultivars span a vast array of colors, sizes and flower forms, but breeders are still working on developing true-blue, scented and frost-hardy selections.

Flowering Onion
Allium

A. *giganteum* (above), A. *cernuum* (below)

Although Allium *leaves release an onion scent when bruised, the flowers are often sweetly fragrant.*

Flowering onions, with their striking, ball-like to loose, nodding clusters of flowers, are sure to attract attention.

Growing

Flowering onions grow best in **full sun**. The soil should be **average to fertile, moist** and **well drained**. Plant bulbs in fall, 2–4" deep, depending on the size of the bulb.

Tips

Flowering onions are best planted in groups in a bed or border where they can be left to naturalize. Most self-seed when left to their own devices. The foliage, which tends to fade just as the plants come into flower, can be hidden with groundcover or a low, bushy companion plant.

Recommended

Several flowering onion species, hybrids and cultivars have gained popularity for their decorative pink, purple, white, yellow, blue or maroon flowers.

A. aflatunense has dense, globe-like clusters of lavender flowers.

A. caeruleum (blue globe onion) produces globe-like clusters of blue flowers.

A. cernuum (nodding or wild onion) delivers loose, drooping clusters of pink flowers.

A. giganteum (giant onion) is a big plant, up to 6' tall, with large, globe-shaped clusters of pinky purple flowers.

Also called: ornamental onion
Features: summer flowers in pink, purple, white, yellow, blue or maroon; cylindrical or strap-shaped leaves **Height:** 12"–6'
Spread: 2–12" **Hardiness:** zones 3–9

Lily
Lilium

Decorative clusters of large, richly colored blooms grace these tall plants. By planting an assortment of cultivars with different blooming times, you can have lilies blooming all season.

Growing

Lilies grow best in **full sun** but like to have their **roots shaded**. The soil should be rich in **organic matter, fertile, moist** and **well drained**. Lily bulbs are best planted in fall before the first frost but can also be planted in spring if bulbs are available.

Tips

Lilies are often grouped in beds and borders, and can be naturalized in woodland gardens and near water features. Group at least three of these tall, narrow plants together to create some volume.

Recommended

The many species, hybrids and cultivars available are grouped by type. Visit your local garden center to see what is available. The following are two popular groups of lilies

Asiatic hybrids bear clusters of flowers in early or mid-summer and are available in a wide range of colors.

Oriental hybrids bear clusters of large, fragrant flowers in mid- and late summer. The usual colors are white, pink or red.

Asiatic hybrids (above), 'Stargazer' (below)

Despite their exotic appearance, lilies are tough and hardy plants that add a wide range of bright colors to the garden.

Features: early, mid- or late-season flowers, in shades of orange, yellow, peach, pink, purple, red, white **Height:** 24–60"
Spread: 12" **Hardiness:** zones 4–8

Tulip

Tulipa

*T*ulips, with their beautiful, often garishly colored flowers, are a welcome sight in the warm days of spring.

Growing

Tulips grow best in **full sun;** in light or partial shade, the flowers tend to bend toward the light. The soil should be **fertile** and **well drained**. Plant the bulbs in fall, 4–6" deep, depending on size of bulb (see planting instruction for daffodils). Bulbs that have been cold treated can be planted in spring. Although tulips can repeat bloom, many hybrids perform best if planted new each year.

Tips

Tulips provide the best display when mass planted or planted in groups in flowerbeds and borders. They can also be grown in containers and can be forced to bloom early in pots indoors. Some of the species and older cultivars can be naturalized in meadow and wildflower gardens.

Recommended

About 100 species of tulips exist. The thousands of hybrids and cultivars are generally divided into 15 groups, according to bloom time and flower appearance. Tulips come in dozens of shades, except blue, and many bicolored or multi-colored varieties are available. Check with your local garden center in early fall for the best selection.

Features: spring flowers in dozens of shades **Height:** 6–30" **Spread:** 2–8" **Hardiness:** zones 3–8; often treated as annuals

Basil

Ocimum

$\mathcal{T}$he sweet, fragrant leaves of fresh basil add a delicious, licorice-like flavor to salads and tomato-based dishes.

Growing

Basil grows best in a **warm, sheltered** location in **full sun**. The soil should be **fertile, moist** and **well drained**. Pinch the tips and remove flower spikes regularly to encourage bushy growth. Plant out or direct sow seed after frost danger has passed in spring.

Tips

Although basil grows best in a warm spot outdoors in the garden, it can be grown successfully in a pot by a bright window indoors to provide you with fresh leaves all year.

Recommended

O. basilicum is one of the most popular of the culinary herbs. There are dozens of varieties, including ones with large or tiny leaves that can be green or purple and smooth or ruffled.

O. b. 'Genovese' and *O. b.* 'Cinnamon' (above)
O. b. 'Genovese' (below)

Basil is a good companion plant for tomatoes—both like warm, moist growing conditions, and when you pick tomatoes for a salad, you'll also remember to include a few sprigs or leaves of basil.

Features: fragrant, decorative leaves
Height: 12–24" **Spread:** 12–18"
Hardiness: tender annual

Chives

Allium

A. schoenoprasum (above & below)

Chives spread with reckless abandon as the clumps grow larger and the plants self-seed.

The delicate onion flavor of chives is best enjoyed fresh. Mix chives into dips or sprinkle them on salads and baked potatoes.

Growing

Chives grow best in **full sun**. The soil should be **fertile, moist** and **well drained,** but chives adapt to most soil conditions. These plants are easy to start from seed, but they do like the soil temperature to stay above 65° F before they germinate, so seeds started directly in the garden are unlikely to sprout before early summer.

Tips

Chives are decorative enough to be included in a mixed or herbaceous border and can be left to naturalize. In an herb garden, chives should be given plenty of space to allow self-seeding.

Recommended

A. schoenoprasum (onion chives) forms a clump of thin, cylindrical, bright green leaves. Clusters of pinky purple flowers are produced in early and mid-summer. Varieties with white or pink flowers are available.

A. tuberosum (garlic chives) produces flat leaves that taste similar to garlic. Attractive white clusters of flowers are produced in mid- to late summer.

Chives are said to increase appetite and encourage good digestion.

Features: long, narrow foliage; clump-forming habit; summer flowers in white, pink or pinky purple **Height:** 8–24" **Spread:** 12" or more **Hardiness:** zones 3–9

Coriander • Cilantro

Coriandrum

Coriander is a multi-purpose herb. The leaves are called cilantro and are used in salads, salsas and soups; the seeds are called coriander and are used in pies, chutneys and marmalades. They both have distinct flavors and culinary uses.

Growing

Coriander prefers **full sun** but tolerates partial shade. The soil should be **fertile, light** and **well drained**. These plants dislike humid conditions and do best during a dry summer. Coriander self-sows if the seeds are left on the surface of the soil or covered lightly with soil.

Tips

Coriander has pungent leaves and is best planted where people do not have to brush past it. It is, however, a delight to behold when in flower. Add a plant or two here and there throughout your borders and vegetable garden, both for the visual appeal and to attract beneficial insects.

Recommended

C. sativum forms a clump of lacy basal foliage above which large, loose clusters of tiny, white flowers are produced. The seeds ripen in late summer and fall.

C. sativum (above & below)

Coriander's delicate, cloud-like clusters of flowers attract pollinating insects such as butterflies and bees as well as predatory insects that help control pest insects.

Features: airy habit; delicate foliage; white summer flowers; decorative seeds
Height: 18–24" **Spread:** 8–18"
Hardiness: tender annual

Dill

Anethum

A. graveolens (above & below)

Probably best known for their use as pickling herbs, dill leaves and seeds have a wide variety of other culinary uses as well.

Growing

Dill grows best in **full sun** in a location **sheltered** from strong winds. The soil should be of **poor to average fertility, moist** and **well drained**. Sow seeds every few weeks in spring and early summer to ensure a regular supply of leaves. Dill should not be grown near fennel or coriander, because cross-pollination will cause the seeds of each plant to lose their distinctive flavors.

Tips

With its feathery leaves, dill is an attractive addition to a mixed bed or border. Dill can be included in a vegetable garden as well. It attracts predatory insects and provides food for swallowtail butterfly larvae.

Recommended

A. graveolens forms a clump of feathery foliage. Clusters of yellow flowers are borne at the tops of sturdy stems.

Dill turns up frequently in historical records as both a culinary and medicinal herb. It was used by the Egyptians and the Romans, and it is mentioned in the Bible.

Features: feathery foliage; yellow summer flowers; striped seeds **Height:** 24–60"
Spread: 12" or more **Hardiness:** annual

Fennel
Foeniculum

All parts of fennel are edible and have a distinctive, licorice-like fragrance and flavor. The seeds are commonly used to make a tea that is good for settling the stomach after a large meal.

Growing
Fennel grows best in **full sun**. The soil should be **average to fertile, moist** and **well drained**. Avoid planting fennel near dill and coriander, because cross-pollination reduces seed production and makes the seed flavor of each less distinct. Fennel easily self-sows.

Tips
Fennel is an attractive addition to a mixed bed or border, and it can be included in a vegetable garden. It also attracts pollinators and predatory insects to the garden. To collect the seeds, remove the seedheads before the seeds start to fall off. It's important to dry them properly before storage to prevent them from getting musty.

Recommended
F. vulgare is a short-lived perennial that forms clumps of loose, feathery foliage. Clusters of small, yellow flowers are borne in late summer. The seeds ripen in fall. **Var. azoricum** (Florence fennel) is a biennial that forms a large, edible bulb at the stem base. This bulb is popular raw in salads, cooked in soups or stews and roasted like other root vegetables. **'Purpureum'** (bronze fennel) is similar in appearance to the species but has bronzy purple foliage.

F. vulgare (above), *F. vulgare* 'Purpureum' (below)

Fennel has been used for its medicinal and culinary properties since before ancient Greek times.

Features: attractive, fragrant foliage; yellow late-summer flowers; decorative seeds; **Height:** 2–6' **Spread:** 12–24" **Hardiness:** zones 4–9

Mint

Mentha

M. x *piperita* (above), decorative variety (below)

A few sprigs of fresh mint added to a pitcher of iced tea gives it an extra zip.

Cool, refreshing mint flavors lend themselves to teas and other hot or cold beverages. Mint sauce made from freshly chopped leaves is often served with lamb.

Growing

Mints grow well in **full sun** or **partial shade**. The soil should be **average to fertile, humus rich** and **moist**. These plants spread vigorously by rhizomes and may need a barrier in the soil to restrict their spread.

Tips

Mints make good groundcovers for damp spots. They grow well along ditches that may be only periodically wet. They can also be used in beds and borders, but they may overwhelm less vigorous plants.

The flowers attract bees, butterflies and other pollinators to the garden.

Recommended

Numerous species, hybrids and cultivars are available. *M. spicata* (spearmint), *M.* x *piperita* (peppermint) and *M.* x *piperata* '**Citrata**' (orange mint) are three of the most commonly grown culinary varieties. More decorative varieties with variegated or curly leaves are also available, as are ones with unusual, fruit-scented foliage.

Features: fragrant, decorative foliage; purple, pink or white summer flowers **Height:** 6–36" **Spread:** 36" or more **Hardiness:** zones 4–8

Oregano • Marjoram

Origanum

O regano and marjoram are two of the best known and most frequently used herbs. They are popular in stuffings, soups and stews, and no pizza is complete until it has been sprinkled with fresh or dried oregano leaves.

Growing

Oregano and marjoram grow best in **full sun**. The soil should be of **poor to average fertility, neutral to alkaline** and **well drained**. The flowers attract pollinators to the garden. Oregano may self-seed.

Tips

These bushy perennials make a lovely addition to any border and can be trimmed to form low hedges.

O. vulgare 'Polyphant' (above), *O. vulgare* 'Aureum' (below)

Recommended

O. majorana (marjoram) is upright and shrubby. It has hairy, light green leaves. and bears white or pink flowers in summer. Where it is not hardy, it can be grown as an annual.

O. vulgare **var.** **hirtum** (oregano, Greek oregano) is the most flavorful culinary variety of oregano. This low, bushy plant has hairy, gray-green leaves and bears white flowers. Many other interesting varieties of *O. vulgare* are available, including those with golden, variegated or curly leaves.

In Greek, oros *means 'mountain' and* ganos *means 'joy,' so oregano translates as 'joy of the mountain.'*

Features: fragrant foliage; white or pink summer flowers; bushy habit **Height:** 12–32"
Spread: 8–18" **Hardiness:** zones 5–9

Parsley
Petroselinum

P. crispum (above), *P. crispum* var. *crispum* (below)

Although often used just as a garnish, parsley is rich in vitamins and minerals and is reputed to freshen the breath after garlic or onion-rich foods are eaten.

Growing
Parsley grows well in **full sun** or **partial shade**. The soil should be of **average to rich fertility, humus rich, moist** and **well drained**. It is best to direct sow the seeds, because the plants resent transplanting. If you do start seeds early, use

Parsley leaves make a tasty and nutritious addition to salads. Tear freshly picked leaves and sprinkle them over or mix them in with your mixed greens.

peat pots so the plants can be potted or planted out without disruption. Parsley is a biennial. Eat the leaves the first year and let a few plants go to seed the second year for manual sowing or self-sowing.

Tips
Containers of parsley can be kept close to the house for easy picking. The bright green leaves and compact growth habit make parsley a good edging plant for beds and borders.

Recommended
P. crispum forms a clump of bright green, divided leaves. This biennial is usually grown as an annual, because it is the leaves that are desired and not flowers or seeds. Cultivars may have flat or curly leaves. Flat leaves are more flavorful and curly ones are more decorative. Dwarf cultivars are also available.

Features: attractive foliage **Height:** 8–24" **Spread:** 12–24" **Hardiness:** zones 5–8; grown as an annual

Rosemary

Rosmarinus

The needle-like leaves of rosemary are used to flavor a wide variety of culinary dishes, including chicken, pork, lamb, rice, tomato and egg dishes.

Growing
Rosemary prefers **full sun** but tolerates partial shade. The soil should be of **poor to average fertility** and **well drained**. These tender shrubs must be moved indoors for winter.

Tips
In Ohio, only a few rosemary cultivars are hardy enough to be used in a shrub border. Here, rosemary is usually planted in a container as a specimen or with other plants and brought indoors for winter. When grown in containers, rosemary rarely reaches its mature size. Low-growing, spreading plants can be included in a rock garden or along the top of a retaining wall, or can be grown in hanging baskets.

Recommended
R. officinalis is a dense, bushy evergreen shrub with narrow, dark green leaves. The habit varies somewhat between cultivars from strongly upright to prostrate and spreading. The flowers are usually in shades of blue, but pink-flowered cultivars are available. Some cultivars can survive in zone 6 in a sheltered location with winter protection.

R. officinalis 'Prostratus' (above), *R. officinalis* (below)

To overwinter a container-grown plant, keep it in a very lightly or partially shaded outdoor site in summer, then put it in a well-ventilated, sunny window indoors for winter. Keep it well watered but allow it to dry out slightly between waterings.

Features: fragrant, evergreen foliage; summer flowers in bright blue or possibly pink
Height: 8"–4' **Spread:** 1–4'
Hardiness: zone (7) 8–10

Sage
Salvia

'Icterina' (above), 'Purpurea' (below)

Sage has been used since at least ancient Greek times as a medicinal and culinary herb and continues to be widely used for both those purposes today.

Sage is perhaps best known as a flavoring for stuffing, but it has a great range of uses and is often added to soups, stews, sausages and dumplings.

Growing
Sage prefers **full sun** but tolerates light shade. The soil should be of **average fertility** and **well drained**. This plant benefits from a light mulch of compost each year. Once established, sage tolerates drought.

Tips
Sage is an attractive plant for the border, adding volume to the middle of the border or as an attractive edging or feature plant near the front. Sage can also be grown in mixed planters.

Recommended
S. officinalis is a woody, mounding plant with soft, gray-green leaves. Spikes of light purple flowers appear in early and mid-summer. Many cultivars with attractive foliage are available, including the silver-leaved 'Berggarten,' the yellow-margined 'Icterina,' the purple-leaved 'Purpurea,' and the variegated 'Tricolor,' which is purple, green and cream, has a pink flush to new growth and is marginally hardy in zone 5.

Features: fragrant, decorative foliage; blue or purple summer flowers **Height:** 12–24" **Spread:** 18–36" **Hardiness:** zones 5–8

Savory
Satureja

S. montana

S. hortensis

The savories are strong, peppery flavored herbs. Well known for flavoring salami, they are added to a wide variety of vegetable and meat dishes. Summer savory is considered to have the most refined flavor of the two savories.

Growing
Savories grow best in **full sun**. The soil should be of **poor to average fertility, neutral to alkaline** and **well drained**. The flowers attract bees, butterflies and other pollinators to the garden.

Features: aromatic foliage; white, pink or purple summer flowers **Height:** 10–16" **Spread:** 8–12" **Hardiness:** zones 5–8 or annual

Tips
These low-growing plants are attractive in the front of beds and borders. They don't like too much moisture in their soil, so they are better suited to the rock garden than the vegetable garden unless you have an area set aside for plants that prefer not to be watered too often.

Recommended
S. hortensis (summer savory) is a bushy annual with narrow leaves. It bears white or pink flowers in summer.

S. montana (winter savory) is a semi-evergreen subshrub that is treated like a perennial. It has narrow, dark green leaves that stay on the plant through early winter. Pink or purple flowers are produced for most of summer.

Summer savory leaves are reputed to relieve bee stings when rubbed on the sore spot.

Tarragon
Artemisia

The distinctive licorice flavor of tarragon lends itself to a wide variety of meat and vegetable dishes and is the key flavoring in Bernaise sauce.

Growing
Tarragon grows best in **full sun**. The soil should be **average to fertile, moist** and **well drained**. Divide the plants every few years to keep them growing vigorously and to encourage the best leaf flavor.

Tips
Tarragon is not exceptionally decorative. It can be included in an herb garden or mixed border where its tall stems will be supported by the surrounding plants.

Recommended
A. dracunculus **var**. *sativa* is a bushy plant with tall stems and narrow leaves. Airy clusters of insignificant flowers are produced in late summer.

A. d. var. sativa (above & below)

Before purchasing a plant, chew a leaf to see if it has the distinctive flavor you seek. French tarragon is the preferred culinary selection, whereas Russian tarragon (A.d. var. dracunculoides*) is a more vigorous plant but has little of the desired flavor.*

Features: narrow, fragrant leaves; airy flowers **Height:** 18–36" **Spread:** 12–18" **Hardiness:** zones 3–8

Thyme

Thymus

Thyme is a popular culinary herb used in the cooking of soups, stews, casseroles and roasts.

Growing

Thyme prefers **full sun**. The soil should be **neutral to alkaline** and of **poor to average fertility**. **Good drainage** is essential. It is beneficial to work leaf mold and sharp limestone gravel into the soil to improve structure and drainage.

Tips

Thyme is useful for sunny, dry locations at the front of borders, between or beside paving stones, on rock gardens and rock walls and in containers.

Once the plants have finished flowering, shear them back by about half to encourage new growth and prevent the plants from becoming too woody.

Recommended

T. **x** *citriodorus* (lemon-scented thyme) forms a mound of lemon-scented, dark green foliage. The summer flowers are pale pink. Cultivars with silver- or gold-margined leaves are available.

T. vulgaris (common thyme) forms a bushy mound of dark green leaves. The summer flowers may be purple, pink or white. Cultivars with variegated leaves are available.

T. vulgaris (above), *T.* x *citriodorus* (below)

Thyme plants are bee magnets when blooming. Pleasantly herbal, thyme honey goes very well with biscuits.

Features: bushy habit; fragrant, decorative foliage; purple, pink or white summer flowers
Height: 8–16" **Spread:** 8–16"
Hardiness: zones 4–9

Ajuga
Ajuga

A. x *tenorii* 'Chocolate Chip' (above), A. *reptans* 'Caitlin's Giant' (below)

Why have grass when you can cover the ground with these lovely ramblers? Often described as rampant runners, ajugas grow best where they can roam freely.

Growing

Ajugas develop the best leaf color in **partial or light shade** but tolerate full shade; excessive sun may scorch the leaves. Any **well-drained** soil is suitable. Divide these vigorous plants any time during the growing season.

When growing hybrids with fancy leaf coloration, remove any new growth or seedlings that revert to green.

Tips

Ajugas make excellent groundcovers for difficult sites, such as exposed slopes and dense shade. They are also attractive in shrub borders, where their dense growth prevents the spread of all but the most tenacious weeds.

Recommended

A. genevensis (Geneva bugleweed) is an upright, noninvasive species that bears blue, white or pink spring flowers.

A. pyramidalis 'Metallica Crispa' (upright bugleweed) is a very slow-growing plant with bronzy, crinkly foliage and violet-blue flowers.

A. reptans is a low, quick-spreading groundcover. The many cultivars are grown for their colorful, often-variegated foliage.

A x tenorii is a hybrid with a finer leaf texture, a very short habit and deep blue flowers. Look for the cultivars **'Chocolate Chip'** and **'Vanilla Chip.'**

Also called: bugleweed **Features:** purple, pink, bronze, green, white or variegated foliage; late-spring to early-summer flowers in purple, blue, pink or white **Height:** 3–12" **Spread:** 6–36" **Hardiness:** zones 3–8

Artemisia

Artemisia

Most artemisias are valued for their silvery foliage, not their flowers. Because it enhances any other hue placed with it, silver is the ultimate blending color.

Growing

Artemisias grow best in **full sun.** The soil should be of **low to average fertility** and **well drained**. These plants dislike wet, humid conditions.

Artemisias respond well to **late-spring pruning,** but don't cut them back too early, or frost may kill the new growth. When they begin to look straggly, they can be cut back to encourage new growth and a neater form. Divide artemisias every year or two, when the plants appear to be thinning in the centers.

Tips

Use artemisias in rock gardens and borders. Their silvery gray foliage makes them good backdrop plants to use behind brightly colored flowers. They are also useful for filling in spaces between other plants. Smaller forms may be used to create knot gardens.

Recommended

A. *ludoviciana* (white sage, silver sage) is an upright, clump-forming plant with silvery white foliage. The species is not grown as often as its cultivars. (Zones 4–8)

A. x **'Powis Castle'** is a compact, mounding, shrubby plant with feathery, silvery gray foliage. This hybrid is reliably hardy to zone 6, but it can also grow in colder

A. *ludoviciana* 'Silver King' (above)
A. *ludoviciana* 'Valerie Finnis' (below)

regions if provided with winter protection in a sheltered site.

A. *schmidtiana* (silvermound artemisia) is a low, dense, mound-forming perennial with feathery, hairy, silvery gray foliage. **'Nana'** (dwarf silvermound) is very compact and grows only half the size of the species.

Also called: wormwood, sage
Features: silvery gray, feathery or deeply lobed foliage **Height:** 6"–6' **Spread:** 12–36"
Hardiness: zones 3–8

Christmas Fern

Polystichum

P. acrostichoides (above & below)

Providing greenery all year, not just during the Christmas season, this native, evergreen fern is a treat. The stocking-shaped leaflets or pinnules are a key identification feature.

Growing

Christmas fern grows well in **partial shade, light shade** or **full shade**. The soil should be **fertile, humus rich** and **moist**. Remove dead and withered fronds in spring before the new ones fill in.

Tips

Christmas fern makes an attractive addition to shaded beds and borders and can be included in a woodland garden. If you have a pond, plant this fern in a moist, shaded area nearby.

Recommended

P. acrostichoides forms a circular cluster of evergreen fronds. It is native to eastern North America.

Hardy, low-growing Christmas fern is less invasive than many of its fern cousins.

Features: evergreen foliage **Height:** 12–18"
Spread: 12–36" **Hardiness:** zones 3–9

Coleus
Solenostemon (Coleus)

There is a coleus for everyone. From brash yellows, oranges and reds to deep maroon and rose selections, the colors, textures and variations are almost limitless.

Growing
Coleus prefers **light** or **partial shade,** but it tolerates full shade that isn't too dense, and it tolerates full sun if watered regularly. The soil should be of **rich** to **average fertility, humus rich, moist** and **well drained.**

Put the seeds in a refrigerator for one or two days to assist in breaking their dormancy. Then place them on the surface of the soil, because they need light to germinate. Green at first, the seedlings develop leaf variegation as they mature.

Tips
The bold, colorful foliage of coleus makes a dramatic impact when the plants are grouped together as edging plants or in beds, borders or mixed containers. Coleus can also be grown indoors as a houseplant in a bright room.

Coleus tends to stretch out and become less attractive after flowering. Prevention is as simple as pinching off the flower buds as they develop.

Recommended
S. scutellarioides (*Coleus blumei* var. *verschaffeltii*) forms a bushy mound of foliage. The leaf edges range from slightly toothed to very ruffled. The leaves are usually multi-colored, with shades ranging from pale greenish yellow to deep

S. s. cultivars (above & below)

purple-black. Hundreds of cultivars are available, but many must be started from cuttings instead of seed.

Coleus can be trained to grow into a standard (tree) form by pinching off the side branches as the plant grows. Once the plant reaches the desired height, pinch from the top to encourage bushy growth.

Features: brightly colored foliage; light purple flowers **Height:** 6–36" **Spread:** usually equal to height **Hardiness:** annual

Dead Nettle

Lamium

L. maculatum 'Anne Greenaway' (above)
L. maculatum 'Beacon Silver' (below)

These attractive plants, with their striped, dotted or banded, silver-and-green foliage, hug the ground and thrive on only the barest necessities of life.

Growing
Dead nettles prefer **partial to light shade;** although they tolerate full sun, they may become leggy. The soil should be of **average fertility, humus rich, moist** and **well drained**. The more fertile the soil, the more vigorously the plants grow. When grown in the shade, these plants tolerate drought, but they can develop bare patches if the soil is allowed to dry out for extended periods. Divide and replant in autumn if any bare spots become unsightly.

Dead nettles remain more compact if sheared back after flowering. If they remain green over winter, shear back in early spring.

Tips
These plants make useful groundcovers for woodland or shade gardens. They also work well under shrubs in a border, where the dead nettles help keep weeds down.

Recommended
L. galeobdolon (*Lamiastrum galeobdolon;* yellow archangel) can be quite invasive, although the several available cultivars are less so. The yellow flowers appear from spring to early summer.

L. maculatum (spotted dead nettle) is the most commonly grown dead nettle. This low-growing, spreading species has green leaves with white or silvery markings and bears white, pink or mauve flowers. Many cultivars are available.

Also called: lamium **Features:** decorative, often variegated foliage; spring or summer flowers in white, pink, yellow or mauve **Height:** 4–24" **Spread:** indefinite **Hardiness:** zones 3–8

Dusty Miller

Senecio

S. *cineraria* 'Cirrus' (above), S. *cineraria* (below)

Dusty miller makes an artful addition to planters, window boxes and mixed borders. The soft, silvery gray, deeply lobed foliage makes a good backdrop to show off the brightly colored flowers of other plants.

Growing
Dusty miller prefers **full sun** but tolerates light shade. The soil should be of **average fertility** and **well drained**.

Tips
This plant's soft, silvery, lacy foliage is its main feature. Dusty miller is used primarily as an edging plant, but it is also useful in beds, borders and containers.

The flowers aren't showy, so most people pinch them off the before they bloom to stop them from using energy that would otherwise go to producing more foliage.

Recommended
S. cineraria forms a mound of fuzzy, silvery gray, lobed or finely divided foliage. Many cultivars with impressive leaf colors and shapes have been developed.

Mix dusty miller with geraniums, begonias or celosias to bring out the vibrant colors of those flowers.

Features: silvery foliage; neat habit; insignificant yellow to cream flowers **Height:** 12–24"
Spread: equal to height or slightly narrower
Hardiness: annual

Flowering Fern
Osmunda

O. regalis (above), O. cinnamomea (below)

The flowering fern's 'flowers' are actually its spore-producing sporangia.

Possessing a certain prehistoric mystique, ferns can add a graceful elegance and textural accent to the garden.

Growing

Flowering ferns prefer **light shade** but tolerate full sun if the soil is consistently moist. The soil should be **fertile, humus rich, acidic** and **moist,** but wet soil is tolerated. Flowering ferns spread as offsets form at the plant bases.

Tips

These large ferns form an attractive mass when planted in large colonies. They can be included in beds and borders. Flowering ferns also make a welcome addition to a woodland garden.

Recommended

O. cinnamomea (cinnamon fern) has light green sterile fronds that fan out in a circular fashion from a central point. Standing straight up in the center of the plant, the leafless, bright green fertile fronds appear in spring; they mature to cinnamon brown.

O. regalis (royal fern) forms a dense clump of foliage. Feathery and flower-like, the rusty brown fertile fronds stand out among the sterile fronds in summer. **'Purpurescens'** has purple-red sterile fronds that mature to green, contrasting with the purple stems. (Zones 3–9)

Features: perennial deciduous fern; decorative fertile fronds; habit **Height:** 30"–5' **Spread:** 2–3' **Hardiness:** zones 2–9

Heuchera

Heuchera

From soft yellow-greens and oranges to midnight purples and silvery, dappled maroons, heucheras offer a great variety of foliage options for a perennial garden with partial shade.

Growing

Heucheras grow best in **light or partial shade;** full sun can bleach out the foliage colors, and the plants grow leggy in full shade. The soil should be of **average to rich fertility, humus rich, neutral to alkaline, moist** and **well drained.** Good air circulation is essential. Deadhead to prolong the bloom. Every two or three years, heucheras should be dug up and the oldest, woodiest roots and stems removed. The plants may be divided at this time, if desired, then replanted with the crown at or just above soil level.

Tips

Use heucheras as edging plants or as groundcovers for low-traffic areas or put them in woodland gardens. They look good in clusters. Combine different foliage types for an interesting display.

Recommended

Dozens of beautiful cultivars offer almost limitless variations of foliage markings and colors. See your local garden center or mail-order catalogue to see what is available.

H. x brizoides 'Firefly' (above), H. sanguineum (below)

Because of their shallow root systems, heucheras have a strange habit of pushing themselves up out of the soil. Mulch the plants in autumn if they begin heaving from the ground.

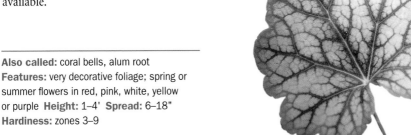

Also called: coral bells, alum root
Features: very decorative foliage; spring or summer flowers in red, pink, white, yellow or purple **Height:** 1–4' **Spread:** 6–18"
Hardiness: zones 3–9

Licorice Plant

Helichrysum

H. petiolare 'Silver' (above), *H. petiolare* 'Limelight' (below)

The silvery sheen of licorice plant, caused by a fine, soft pubescence on its leaves, makes it a perfect complement for many other plants.

Growing

Licorice plant prefers **full sun**. The soil should be of **poor to average fertility, neutral** or **alkaline** and **well drained**. Licorice plant wilts when the soil dries but revives quickly once watered. If it

Licorice plant is a good indicator plant for hanging baskets. When it starts looking wilted, it is time to water.

outgrows its space, snip it back to a leaf node using a pair of pruners, shears or even scissors.

Tips

Prized for its foliage rather than its flowers, licorice plant is a tender perennial grown as an annual. Include it in your hanging baskets, planters and window boxes to provide a soft, silvery backdrop for the colorful flowers of other plants. Licorice plant can also be used as a groundcover in beds, borders and rock gardens, and along the tops of retaining walls.

Recommended

H. petiolare is a trailing plant with fuzzy, gray-green leaves. Cultivars are more common than the species and include varieties with lime green, silver or variegated leaves.

Features: trailing habit; colorful, fuzzy foliage **Height:** 20" **Spread:** about 36"; sometimes up to 6' **Hardiness:** annual

Little Bluestem

Schizachyrium

One of our native grasses, little bluestem is more tolerant than other Ohio natives of the poor soils that often surround new homes. Its upright habit lends a touch of the prairie to the garden.

Growing

Little bluestem grows best in **full sun**. The soil should be of **average fertility** and **well drained**. Too much fertility can cause little bluestem to 'lodge' or flop over. Cut the stems back in late fall or early spring.

Tips

This drought-resistant native grass naturalizes well and easily self-seeds. It makes a useful addition to beds, borders and areas where watering is minimal and the soil drains quickly. The flower plumes are popular for use in dried flower arrangements.

Recommended

S. scorparium (*Andropogon scoparius*) forms a clump of narrow, blue-green foliage that turns red-purple, becoming coppery in fall. The plumy, pink flowers of late summer ripen to copper and last through fall.

Features: upright habit; colorful foliage; plumy, pink flowers
Height: 24–36" **Spread:** 12–18"
Hardiness: zones 4–9

S. scorparium

The intensely silver blue leaves of 'The Blues' are electric in the garden.

Lungwort

Pulmonaria

P. saccharata (above & below)

The wide array of lungworts available offer highly attractive foliage that ranges in color from apple green to silver-spotted and olive to dark emerald.

Growing

Lungworts prefer **partial to full shade**. The soil should be **fertile, humus rich, moist** and **well drained**. Rot can occur in very wet soil.

Divide after flowering in early summer or in autumn. Provide the newly planted divisions with lots of water to help them re-establish.

To keep lungworts tidy and to show off the fabulous foliage, deadhead the plants by removing the flower stems after flowering.

Tips

Lungworts are useful and attractive groundcovers for shady borders, woodland gardens and pond and stream edges.

Recommended

P. longifolia (long-leaved lungwort) forms a dense clump of long, narrow, green leaves with white spots and bears clusters of blue flowers.

P. officinalis (common lungwort, spotted dog) forms a loose clump of evergreen foliage with white spots. The flowers open pink and mature to blue. Cultivars are available.

P. saccharata (Bethlehem sage) forms a compact clump of large, evergreen leaves with white spots and purple, red or white flowers. Many cultivars and hybrids with other lungwort species are available.

Features: decorative, mottled or spotted foliage; blue, red, pink or white spring flowers **Height:** 8–24" **Spread:** 8–36" **Hardiness:** zones 3–8

Miscanthus

Miscanthus

Miscanthus is one of the most popular and majestic of all the ornamental grasses. Its graceful foliage dances in the wind and is an impressive sight all year long.

Growing

Miscanthus prefers **full sun**. The soil should be of **average fertility**, **moist** and **well drained,** although some selections tolerate wet soil. All selections tolerate drought once established.

Tips

Give this magnificent beauty room to spread so you can fully appreciate its form. This grass creates dramatic impact in groups or as seasonal screens. The height of each selection determines the best place for it in the border.

Miscanthus has become invasive in some places, so check with your local agricultural extension agent for current information for your area.

Recommended

M. sinensis offers numerous cultivars, all distinguished by the white midrib on the leaf blade. Some popular selections include **'Gracillimus'** (maiden grass), with long, fine-textured leaves; **'Grosse Fontaine'** (large fountain), a tall, wide-spreading, early-flowering selection; **'Morning Light'** (variegated maiden grass), a short and delicate plant with fine, white leaf edges; **var. purpurescens** (flame grass), with foliage that turns

M. sinensis var. *purpurescens* (above)
W. sinensis cultivar (below)

bright orange in early fall; and **'Strictus'** (porcupine grass), a tall, stiff, upright selection with unusual horizontal yellow bands.

Also called: eulalia, Japanese silver grass
Features: upright, arching habit; colorful summer and fall foliage; pink, copper or silver flowers in late summer and fall; winter interest
Height: 4–8' **Spread:** 2–4'
Hardiness: zones 5–9, possibly zone 4

Pachysandra

Pachysandra

P. terminalis (above & below)

The low-maintenance pachysandras are among the most popular groundcovers around. The rhizomatous rootzone of these plants colonizes quickly to form a dense blanket of leaves over the ground.

Growing

Pachysandras prefer **light to full shade** and tolerate partial shade. Any soil that is **moist, acidic, humus rich** and **well drained** is good. Propagation is easy with cuttings or by division.

Tips

Pachysandras are durable groundcovers under trees, in shady borders and in woodland gardens. The foliage is considered evergreen, but winter-scorched shoots may need to be removed in spring. Shear or mow old plantings in early spring to rejuvenate them.

Recommended

P. procumbens (Allegheny spurge) is our native pachysandra. Although slow to establish, it is worth the wait. Its bold texture at ground level adds a lush feel to the woodland garden.

P. terminalis (Japanese Spurge) forms a low mass of foliage rosettes that can spread almost indefinitely. **'Green Sheen'** is named for its exceptionally glossy leaves, which are smaller than those of the species. **'Variegata'** has white margins or mottled, silver foliage, but it is not as vigorous as the species.

Also called: Japanese Spurge
Features: perennial, evergreen groundcover; low, spreading habit; fragrant, inconspicuous, white flowers in spring **Height:** 8"
Spread: 12–18" or more
Hardiness: zones 3–9

Painted Fern • Lady Fern
Athyrium

A. niponicum var. *pictum* (above & below)

These ferns are some of the most well-behaved ferns, adding color and texture to shady spots without growing rampantly out of control.

Growing
These ferns grow well in **full shade, partial shade** or **light shade**. The soil should be of **average fertility, humus rich, acidic** and **moist**. Division is rarely required but can be done to propagate more plants.

Tips
Lady ferns and painted ferns form an attractive mass of foliage but without growing out of control the way some ferns tend to. Include them in shade gardens and moist woodland gardens.

Recommended
A. filix-femina (lady fern) forms a dense clump of lacy fronds. The available cultivars include dwarf varieties and plants with variable foliage.

A. niponicum var. *pictum* 'Metallicum' (Japanese painted fern) forms a clump of dark green fronds with a silvery or reddish metallic sheen. Many other cultivars of *A. niponicum* var. *pictum* with differing colors of foliage are available. (Zones 4–8)

With its metallic shades of silver, burgundy and bronze, the colorful foliage of the Japanese painted fern will brighten up any shaded area.

Features: clumping habit; lacy, sometimes-colorful foliage **Height:** 12–24"
Spread: 12–24" **Hardiness:** zones 3–9

Persian Shield

Strobilanthes

S. *dyerianus* (above & below)

Persian shield's iridescent foliage in shades of purple, bronze, silver and pink adds a bright touch to any annual planting.

Growing

Persian shield grows well in **full sun** or **partial shade**. The soil should be **average to fertile, light** and **very well drained**. Pinch the growing tips to encourage

Persian shield can be overwintered indoors in a cool, bright location.

bushy growth. Cuttings can be started in late summer and overwintered indoors.

Tips

The colorful foliage of Persian shield provides a dramatic background in annual or mixed beds and borders or in container plantings. Combine this plant with yellow- or white-flowered plants for stunning contrast.

Recommended

S. dyerianus forms a mound of silver- or purple-flushed foliage with contrasting dark green, bronze or purple veins and margins. Spikes of blue flowers may appear in early fall.

Features: decorative foliage **Height:** 18–36"
Spread: 24–36" **Hardiness:** tender shrub, treated as an annual

Reed Grass
Calamagrostis

This graceful metamorphic grass changes its habit and flower color with the seasons. The slightest breeze sets this grass in motion.

Growing

Reed grass grows best in **full sun**. The soil should be **fertile, moist** and **well drained**. Heavy clay and dry soils are tolerated, but this plant may be susceptible to rust during cool, wet summers or in sites with poor air circulation. Rain and heavy snow may cause it to flop temporarily, but it quickly bounces back. Cut reed grass back to 2–4" in very early spring, before growth begins, and divide it if it begins to die out in the center.

Tips

Whether it's used as a single, stately focal point, in small groupings or in large drifts, reed grass is a desirable, low-maintenance plant. It combines well with perennials that bloom in late summer and fall.

Recommended

C. x *acutiflora* '**Karl Foerster'** (Foerster's feather reed grass), the most popular selection, forms a loose mound of green foliage from which the airy, bottlebrush flowers emerge in June. The flowering stems have a loose, arching habit when they first emerge, but they grow more stiff and upright over summer. Watch for a recent introduction called '**Avalanche,'** which has a white center stripe. Another cultivar is '**Overdam,'** a compact, less hardy selection with white leaf edges.

'Overdam' (above), 'Karl Foerster' (below)

If you like the way reed grass holds its flowers high above its mounded foliage, consider Deschampsia *(tufted hair grass) and* Molinia *(moor grass) species and cultivars. Some have foliage with creamy yellow stripes.*

Features: open habit, becoming upright; silvery pink flowers that turn rich tan; green, possibly white-striped foliage that turns bright gold in fall; winter interest **Height:** 3–5' **Spread:** 2–3' **Hardiness:** zones 4–9

Sea Oats

Chasmanthium

C. latifolium (above & below)

This native grass is at home in our moist, shady woodlands, but its bamboo-like foliage gives it a tropical flair.

Growing

Sea oats thrives in **full shade to full sun,** although its habit relaxes in deep shade. The soil should be **fertile** and **moist;** dry soils are tolerated, but plants in full sun must be kept moist to prevent leaf scorch. Divide to control the rapid spread. Cut this plant back early each spring to 2" above the ground. The seedlings of this vigorous self-seeder are easily removed and composted or shared with friends.

Tips

Sea oats is a tremendous plant for moist, shady areas. Its upright, arching habit when in full bloom makes it attractive alongside a stream or pond, in a large drift or in a container.

Recommended

C. latifolium forms a spreading clump of unusual, bright green, bamboo-like foliage. The scaly, dangling spikelet flowers arrange themselves nicely on delicate stems just slightly above the foliage. In fall, the foliage turns bronze, and the flowers turn gold.

Also called: northern sea oats
Features: bamboo-like foliage; unusual flowers; winter interest **Height:** 32"–4'
Spread: 18–24" **Hardiness:** zones 5-9

Sensitive Fern
Onoclea

O. sensibilis (above & below)

A common sight along stream banks and in wooded areas of Ohio, this native fern thrives in moist and shaded conditions.

Growing

Sensitive fern grows best in **light shade** but tolerates full shade or partial shade; too much sun can scorch the fronds. The soil should be **fertile, humus rich** and **moist**, although some drought is tolerated. Late spring or early fall frosts can easily damage this plant.

Tips

Sensitive fern likes damp, shady places. Include it in shaded borders, woodland gardens and other locations with protection from the wind.

Recommended

O. sensibilis forms a mass of light green, deeply lobed, arching fronds. Fertile fronds are produced in late summer and persist through winter. The spores are produced in structures that look like black beads, which give the fertile fronds a decorative appearance and make them a popular addition to floral arrangements.

This fern is reputed to tolerate the toxins produced by the black walnut (Juglans nigra), making it a good choice for planting beneath this tree.

Features: deciduous perennial fern; attractive foliage; arching habit **Height:** 24"
Spread: indefinite **Hardiness:** zones 4–9

Sweet Potato Vine

Ipomoea

I. b. 'Tricolor' (above), *I.b.* 'Margarita' (below)

This vigorous, rambling plant has leaves that can be pink and cream variegated, lime green or a bruise-like purple or green. Sweet potato vine grows so easily it can make any gardener look like a genius.

Growing

Grow sweet potato vine in **full sun**. A **light**, **well-drained** soil of **poor fertility** is preferred, but any type will do. Container-grown plants can be overwintered in a greenhouse or other bright location.

Tips

Sweet potato vine is a great addition to mixed planters, window boxes and hanging baskets. It scrambles about in rock gardens and cascades down over the edges of retaining walls. Although this plant is a vine, its bushy habit and colorful leaves make it a useful foliage plant.

Recommended

I. batatas is a twining climber that is grown for its attractive foliage rather than its flowers. Several cultivars are available.

As a bonus, when you pull up your sweet potato vine at the end of summer, you can eat any tubers that have formed, or you can store them in a cold, dry location to grow the following year.

Features: decorative foliage **Height:** about 12" **Spread:** up to 10' **Hardiness:** tender annual tuber

Sweet Woodruff

Galium

G. odoratum (above & below)

Sweet woodruff is a groundcover with many good qualities, including attractive light green foliage that smells like freshly mown hay, abundant white flowers in spring and the ability to fill in garden spaces without taking over.

Growing

This plant prefers **partial shade;** in full shade it grows well but doesn't bloom well. The soil should be **humus rich, slightly acidic** and **evenly moist.** Sweet woodruff competes successfully with other plant roots and flourishes where some other groundcovers, such as *Vinca,* fail to do so.

Tips

Sweet woodruff makes a perfect woodland groundcover. It forms a beautiful green carpet and loves the same conditions as those in which azaleas and rhododendrons thrive. Interplant it with spring bulbs for a fantastic display in spring.

Recommended

G. odoratum is a low, spreading groundcover. It bears clusters of star-shaped, white flowers in a flush in late spring and then sporadically through mid-summer.

Sweet woodruff's vanilla-scented dried leaves and flowers were once used to scent bed linens and are often added to potpourri. They are also used to flavor beverages, particularly the traditional German May wine.

Features: deciduous, perennial groundcover; white late-spring to mid-summer flowers; fragrant foliage; trailing habit **Height:** 12–18"
Spread: indefinite **Hardiness:** zones 3–8

Switch Grass
Panicum

P. *virgatum* cultivar (above)
P. *virgatum* 'Heavy Metal' (below)

The delicate, airy panicles of switch grass fill gaps in the garden border, and they can be cut for fresh or dried arrangements.

A native to the prairie grasslands, switch grass naturalizes equally well in an informal border or a natural meadow.

Growing

Switch grass thrives in **full sun, light shade** or **part shade**. Although the soil should be of **average fertility** and **well-drained,** this plant adapts to moist or dry soils and tolerates conditions ranging from heavy clay to lighter, sandy soil. Cut switch grass back to 2–4" from the ground in early spring. The flower stems may break under heavy, wet snow or in exposed, windy sites.

Tips

Plant switch grass singly in small gardens, in large groups in spacious borders or, for a dramatic, whimsical effect, at the edges of ponds or pools. The seedheads attract birds, and the foliage changes color in fall, so place this plant where you can enjoy both features.

Recommended

P. virgatum (switch grass) is suited to wild meadow gardens. It has a number of popular cultivars. **'Heavy Metal'** (blue switch grass) is an upright plant with narrow, steely blue foliage flushed with gold and burgundy in fall. **'Prairie Sky'** (blue switch grass) is an arching plant with deep blue foliage. **'Shenandoah'** (red switch grass) has red-tinged, green foliage that turns burgundy in fall.

Features: clumping habit; green, blue or burgundy foliage; airy panicles of flowers; fall color; winter interest **Height:** 3–5' **Spread:** 30–36" **Hardiness:** zones 3–9

Wild Ginger
Asarum

A. canadense (above), *A. europaeum* (below)

The attractive dark green, heart-shaped leaves of wild ginger form a dense mat that suppresses weeds and fills in under trees where sun-loving grass won't grow.

Growing

Wild gingers grow well in **light shade, partial shade** or **full shade**. The soil should be of **average fertility, humus rich, moist** and **acidic,** although *A. canadense* tolerates alkaline conditions. Prolonged drought can cause the plants to wilt and die back.

Tips

Use wild gingers in shady rock gardens, borders or woodland gardens. These plants readily spread to cover the ground, but they are also fairly easy to remove from places where they aren't welcome.

Recommended

A. canadense (Canada wild ginger) is native to the Midwest and eastern North America. The heart-shaped leaves are slightly hairy.

A. europaeum (European wild ginger) is a European species that forms an expanding clump of glossy, silver-veined leaves. It is not as heat-tolerant as *A. canadense.*

The rhizomes of wild ginger have a distinctive gingery scent, and, although they are not related to the culinary ginger (Zingiber officinale), they can be used as a similar flavoring in many dishes.

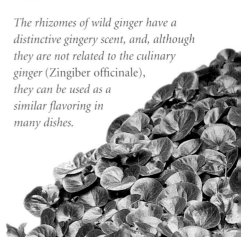

Features: heart-shaped foliage; ginger-scented rhizomes **Height:** 3–6" **Spread:** 12" or more **Hardiness:** zones 4–8

Wood Fern

Dryopteris

D. erythrosora (above)

The lovely wood ferns have several interesting cultivars that provide unusual crinkled or crested fronds.

Growing

Wood ferns grow best in **partial shade,** but they tolerate full sun in wet soil. The soil should be **fertile, humus rich** and **moist**. Divide the plants to control spread and propagate.

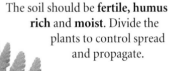

Tips

These large, impressive ferns are useful in shaded areas or woodland gardens. If you have an area of the garden that stays moist or periodically floods, they are an ideal choice.

Recommended

D. filix-mas (male fern) forms a clump of lacy fronds. Cultivars with decorative and sometimes unusual frond variations are available.

D. erythrosora (autumn fern) is named for the bronze to apricot color of its bold leaves in spring and fall.

Wood ferns are among the easiest ferns to grow and among the hardiest.

Features: decorative fronds **Height:** 30"–4'
Spread: 24–36" **Hardiness:** zones 3–8

Glossary

Acid soil: soil with a pH lower than 7.0

Annual: a plant that germinates, flowers, sets seed and dies in one growing season

Alkaline soil: soil with a pH higher than 7.0

Basal leaves: leaves that form from the crown, at the base of the plant

Bract: a modified leaf at the base of a flower or flower cluster

Corm: a bulb-like, food-storing, underground stem, resembling a bulb without scales

Crown: the part of the plant at or just below soil level where the shoots join the roots

Cultivar: a cultivated plant variety with one or more distinct differences from the species, e.g., in flower color or disease resistance

Damping off: fungal disease causing seedlings to rot at soil level and topple over

Deadhead: to remove spent flowers to maintain a neat appearance and encourage a longer blooming season

Direct sow: to sow seeds directly in the garden

Dormancy: a period of plant inactivity, usually during winter or unfavorable conditions

Double flower: a flower with an unusually large number of petals

Genus: a category of biological classification between the species and family levels; the first word in a scientific name indicates the genus

Grafting: a type of propagation in which a stem or bud of one plant is joined onto the rootstock of another plant of a closely related species

Hardy: capable of surviving unfavorable conditions, such as cold weather or frost, without protection

Hip: the fruit of a rose, containing the seeds

Humus: decomposed or decomposing organic material in the soil

Hybrid: a plant resulting from natural or human-induced cross-breeding between varieties, species or genera

Inflorescence: a flower cluster

Male clone: a plant that may or may not produce pollen but that will not produce fruit, seed or seedpods

Neutral soil: soil with a pH of 7.0

Perennial: a plant that takes three or more years to complete its life cycle

pH: a measure of acidity or alkalinity; the soil pH influences availability of nutrients for plants

Rhizome: a root-like, food-storing stem that grows horizontally at or just below soil level, from which new shoots may emerge

Rootball: the root mass and surrounding soil of a plant

Seedhead: dried, inedible fruit that contains seeds; the fruiting stage of the inflorescence

Self-seeding: reproducing by means of seeds without human assistance, so that new plants constantly replace those that die

Semi-double flower: a flower with petals in two or three rings

Single flower: a flower with a single ring of typically four or five petals

Species: the fundamental unit of biological classification; the entity from which cultivars and varieties are derived

Standard: a shrub or small tree grown with an erect main stem, accomplished either through pruning and training or by grafting the plant onto a tall, straight stock

Sucker: a shoot that comes up from the root, often some distance from the plant; it can be separated to form a new plant once it develops its own roots

Tender: incapable of surviving the climatic conditions of a given region and requiring protection from frost or cold

Tuber: the thick section of a rhizome bearing nodes and buds

Variegation: foliage that has more than one color, often patched or striped or bearing leaf margins of a different color

Variety: a naturally occurring variant of a species

Index of Recommended Species Plant Names

Entries in **bold** type indicate main plant headings.